WHAT EVERY COUPLE SHOULD KNOW...

IN BED TOGETHER

GRAHAM MASTERTON

author of
HOW TO DRIVE YOUR MAN WILD IN BED

SIGNET • 451-AE7212 • (CANADA $6.99) • U.S. $5.99

BECOME THE LOVER
OF YOUR MATE'S FANTASIES

The reassuring truth about lovemaking is
that your partner is somebody you love
and trust and who loves and trusts you in
return. With that trust in place, erotic
ecstasy can be yours as you sex each other
to the max, night after fabulous night.
This sensational guide outlines a step-by-
step program that will take you beyond
your wildest imagination to the most
fantastic sex you've ever dreamed about.
You will learn:

*Your hidden sex potential
*How to bare your all
*The look of love
*The rewards of super-stimulation
*And 18 different ways to enjoy
 the thrill of it all

WILD IN BED
TOGETHER

GRAHAM MASTERTON is the author of
some of the most popular sex manuals
of all time and is a former editor for
Penthouse, *Mayfair*, and *Penthouse Forum*
magazines. He is married and lives with
his wife and three sons in England.

WILD
IN BED
TOGETHER

Graham Masterton

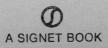

A SIGNET BOOK

SIGNET
Published by the Penguin Group
Penguin Books USA Inc., 375 Hudson Street,
New York, New York 10014, U.S.A.
Penguin Books Ltd, 27 Wrights Lane,
London W8 5TZ, England
Penguin Books Australia Ltd, Ringwood,
Victoria, Australia
Penguin Books Canada Ltd, 10 Alcorn Avenue,
Toronto, Ontario, Canada M4V 3B2
Penguin Books (N.Z.) Ltd, 182–190 Wairau Road,
Auckland 10, New Zealand

Penguin Books Ltd, Registered Offices:
Harmondsworth, Middlesex, England

First published by Signet, an imprint of New American Library,
a division of Penguin Books USA Inc.

First Printing, April, 1992
10 9 8 7 6 5 4 3

PRINTED IN THE UNITED STATES OF AMERICA

For Wiescka
Better Than Ever,
Closer Than Ever

Contents

1

Your Hidden Sex Potential

If I were to tell you that you were making only an eighth of the amount of money of which you were capable, you would be justifiably concerned about what you were doing wrong.

You wouldn't sit idle; you'd want to know what your full money-making potential really was—why you weren't exploiting it—and what you could do to improve your performance as soon as you possibly could.

You're an achiever, after all. People who aren't achievers don't bother to read books that might possibly give them the key to improving their lifestyles.

People who aren't achievers don't care in the same way you do about reaching for the peaks of personal success. And we're not just talking about success in money-making, but in your relationships with others, in your physical and psychological self-development, and in setting and reaching long-term goals.

But *you* care. And that's why—if I were to alter the wording of my first paragraph just a little, and tell you that it wasn't your money-making performance I was talking about, but your *sexual* performance, then obviously you'd be just as eager to find out how you could make things better.

The trouble is that—up until now—there have been no sex manuals that have been specifically designed to help you achieve your peak sexual performance. In the same way that athletes have to train to reach their peak, lovers have to train, too. Not in the same way as a track star, of course—not coldly or mechanically or unemotionally—but in a caring, dedicated, and sensitive way.

How do you train to make love better? Well, you can spend night after night trying out different techniques and discovering what they do for you (or what they *don't*). The problem is, sex is physically and emotionally strenuous. So unlike golf, or squash, or running, or swimming, it's not so easy to practice more than two or three different techniques per night—if that. It could take you *years* to find out by trial and error what turns you on the most.

Or, you can read this book—and learn through other people's experiences what sexual acts excite you the most *and exactly how to train yourself to do them really well*.

This book—based like all of my books on scores of interviews and letters and discussions—brings you the real experiences of dozens of people who have been successful in improving their sexual pleasure. You can use *their* sexual successes in order to achieve your own.

I've often been asked: "What's the good of a *book*? What can a *book* possibly do to improve my sex life?"

It's a fair question. And the answer is that many sex books—although they contain all the fundamental facts about sex, and some sensible suggestions about how to please your partner in bed—*don't* really help you to take your lovemaking right up to the very limit of which you and your partner are capable.

In other words, they don't stretch you.

You may well be content with what you've got. After all, some skiers are content to stay on the nursery slopes. But whoever you are, and whatever your sexual situation—even if you don't have a partner at this particular time in your life—you're capable of much, much more. More satisfaction, more sensation—an evermore adventurous sex life that will always be exciting, and will at times be breathtaking. Guaranteed: provided you're prepared to give it *everything*.

What makes this book different is that it demands that you tax your sexual capabilities to the utmost. It's informative, yes. It's reassuring, too, as any good sex manual should be. But I'm not going to allow you to get away with anything less than your very best shot—every single time you have sex. In fact, I'll insist that you make the earth move, even when you masturbate.

You see, I'm not a clinician or a sexual therapist. I'm not dealing with people who are suffering from any particular sexual dysfunction. I'm helping to guide and train people like you—who are already competent and well-adjusted lovers—to discover that sex can be more than comforting, more than a way of releasing your physical and emotional tensions, more than a way of showing your lover how much you care.

The reason I can insist that you try to make each sex act so stunning is that all of the guidance in this book is based not on cozy, well-meaning theory or women's magazine articles or sex-therapy files. It's based on the real and recent experiences of sexually active men and women who have been striving to improve their sex lives by every means that you can imagine—and then some.

When you read this book, you will to all intents and purposes be a firsthand witness to scores of energetic sex acts by men and women whose instructions were to take their erotic experience to the max. You will be able to visualize what they are doing far more graphically than if you were watching a sex movie, because you will be told what they did, why they did it, what it felt like, what it looked like, and, most important, how you can do it, too.

A movie, for example, can show you a man and a woman enjoying oral sex. But a movie can never portray what it's like for the woman to take her lover's penis into her mouth—*why* she's doing it, whether she enjoys it or not, what it tastes like, how she licks and sucks it, right down to the minutest detail. But when you set out to achieve peak-performance sex, it's precisely those reasons and responses that make all the difference.

Imagine, for example, a movie scene in which a man enters a bedroom, still toweling himself after his shower, to find his young blonde wife lying naked on the bed. He lies down next to her, his penis rising, and kisses her. She pushes him onto his back, kneels beside him, and takes his penis into her mouth, swirling and teasing it with her tongue. At the same time, she caresses his testicles and begins to massage the shaft of his penis up and down. After a while, he groans and shudders, and his wife sits up, wiping her lips with the back of her hand.

Erotic to look at, possibly. But what can such a movie tell you? Have you really learned anything about this couple—why the wife wanted to fellate her husband, whether she genuinely liked it or suffered it just to please him—whether she swallowed his sperm or not—whether she had ever done it before—whether she would ever do it again—how *he* felt about it? Was it satisfying, or was it frustrating? What contribution can oral caresses make to a sexual relationship? Do men enjoy oral sex more than women? What does sperm taste like? Is it harmful/fattening/beneficial? Did this particular woman like the taste of it?

A movie can never answer any of those questions, and neither can most sex manuals. Here, for instance, is a typical discussion about oral sex from the *Encyclopedia of Love & Sex:*

> What are these techniques that cause such comment and confusion? They are a special sort of sexual intercourse in which the man tickles the woman's clitoris and labia minora with his tongue (cunnilingus) while she touches his penis with her lips and her tongue and takes it into her mouth (fellatio). As in all lip and tongue contact there is licking and sucking as well.
>
> The man approaching the woman usually does so while she is lying on her back, legs bent apart. A woman can fellate a man lying down but he may prefer to stand or sit on the side of the bed with the woman kneeling in front of him. If both want to do it simultaneously, they should lie down, head to tail on their sides facing each other, face curved into the genitals in the position known as 69, because that is the shape the two bodies make. (Page 144.)

Of course, anyone who's ever enjoyed 69 will know that trying to do it on your side is one of the most awkward and uncomfortable sexual positions ever invented. The man's head will be trapped between the woman's thighs—unless she's a trained ballerina, and is capable of keeping her leg raised for ten minutes without trembling. Even so his access to her vagina will be ridiculously limited. She needs to open up her cunt as wide as possible, so that he can lick and stimulate her in every crevice of her vagina, her urethra, her labia minora, and her clitoris, as well as her anus.

But apart from that, the *Encyclopedia's* description falls desperately short in many respects. It gives the reader no information about the complex urges behind oral sex, how and why people do it, and what sensations they should expect.

For instance—despite the old joke—Q. "What was the worst blowjob you ever had?" A. "Fantastic!"—many men experience considerably *less* sexual sensation during oral sex than they do during intercourse. While they may be highly stimulated by the sight of their lover sucking and licking their penis, they frequently need quite vigorous hand masturbation as well as tongue stimulation in order to reach a climax.

Sometimes they have conscious or unconscious reservations about ejaculating into their lover's mouth. Sometimes they find themselves inhibited by the fact that they are expected to lie passive and have something done to *them*, instead of the other way around—and some men are unsettled by handing over sexual control to their partners. Mostly, however, the problem is plain old biology. Men have a strong natural urge to climax inside a woman's vagina for the sake of perpetuating the species. For instance, 32-year-old Peter, of St. Louis, told me: "I always had a fantasy about taking my cock out of my wife's cunt and shooting sperm all over her stomach, and then kind of massaging it in. But every time a climax came close, all my body wanted to do was force itself deeper and deeper inside her. My brain may have wanted me to take my cock out, but my body said, no way. I find it real hard to take my cock out of my wife's cunt right at the moment of climax, believe me. That's why I never believed in the withdrawal method. I mean, show me the guy who's got the moral strength to withdraw!"

So—you won't find theoretical descriptions of sex in this manual. Instead, you'll find practical, tried-and-tested acts of erotic stimulation, described in the words of the men and women who have tried and tested them. To put it another way, every suggestion in this book carries the seal of Good Lovemaking.

The Sexual Workout

I'm also frequently asked *why* I expect people to put so much effort into improving their sex lives. As one 27-year-old grade-school teacher from Port Charlotte, Florida, wrote me, "As if I didn't have enough to do, being a working mother, a wife, a cook, a taxi-driver, a laundress, and a swim instructor, you want me to have better orgasms as well!"

Quite frankly, I answered her, yes. Because the benefits of reaching the peak of one's sexual ability can be tremendous, both physically and emotionally. Not just for high-flying young people in first-class athletic shape, but for men and women of all ages and backgrounds and situations. The well-being that you can derive from a fully realized sex life has been shown to help almost everything you do, from work to recreation. If you want to transform your life—and *transform* isn't too dramatic a word to use—there is no better place to start than in the bedroom (or wherever you prefer to make love).

This is 38-year-old Dave, a realtor from Wheaton, Maryland: "It had never occurred to me before I read your last book (*How to Make Love Six Nights a Week*) that I could excite my wife Mary even more than I was doing already. As far as I was concerned, our sex life seemed to be fairly regular and fairly satisfying. The idea that I ought to think about it more and try out new ways of improving it was kind of alien to me. But the more I read, the more logical it seemed. After all, I spend literally hours every week trying to improve my bowling technique, why shouldn't I spend a little time trying to improve my sex technique?"

One of the main reasons, of course, why men *don't* work so hard at improving their lovemaking is because they are loath to admit that they might be in some way lacking when it comes to stimulating their lovers. The big macho bit. Another reason is that they simply don't realize that they *should* be working on their lovemaking, equally hard (if not harder) than their golf swing. After all, what sex-education curriculum makes it clear to boys and girls that good lovemaking doesn't happen by instinct or by accident? Good lovemaking comes from knowledge, understanding, passion, patience—and practice.

The main reason why both men and women don't try to improve their lovemaking, however, is that they simply don't know how—and it isn't particularly easy to learn how. Despite the fact that magazines like *Playboy* and *Penthouse Forum* often include constructive and helpful articles about improving sexual technique, many people are still too embarrassed to buy a "top-shelf" magazine, especially because they are so blatantly published as a stimulus for masturbation.

Dave found what I had written about the female sex organs and how to arouse them to be a revelation. "For the first time, with the help of your book, I persuaded Mary to lie back on the couch with her legs wide apart, so that I could actually *see* what she looked like. I opened up her vaginal lips, caressed her clitoris—fingered her, licked her, *tasted* her—really explored, and took my time about it, too—totally unhurried, so that our excitement could gradually build up, the way you described. It was a revelation for Mary, too, and because I found it such a turn-on, she was turned on, too. By the time I'd finished touching her and examining her, her vagina was shining with juice, and we had what I'd call the first act of intercourse of our new improved love life."

In a similar way, 22-year-old Houston homemaker Katherine discovered the pleasures of her husband's penis. "I guess in a way I'd always been afraid of it. I knew all about sex from lessons at school, but my experience with boys was pretty limited. I lost my virginity when I was just 16, and before I got married to Paul, I'd had three steady boyfriends, I mean boys that I'd gone to bed with.

"But of course I'd never *examined* them. I mean I'd hardly touched them. They put it in and that was it. It never crossed my mind that I ought to know what a cock looked like close-up and how it worked and what it was all about. How many women know that the end of it is much more sensitive than the shaft, or how to hold it properly or how to touch it, or how men like you to rub it? They don't tell you that stuff in school and my mother sure wouldn't have dreamed of telling me anything about 'how to hold a man's cock.' I think she would rather have died.

"But when Paul brought your book home we did spend a whole lot of time discovering each other's bodies, and I guess you could say that I got to know his cock real well and made *very* good friends with it. I'm not afraid to touch it now, or to kiss it. I guess I was scared to, before, because I didn't know whether he'd enjoy it, or whether it would hurt him in any way, or whether he'd think I was behaving like a whore. I mean that goes on in a lot of women's minds, especially if their husband's pretty religious or conventional. They don't want to kiss their cocks or anything because they're afraid their husbands'll think they're sluts—whereas, you know, I expect their husbands would *love* it, in actual fact.

"I've learned to use my hands, and I've learned to use them often. Sometimes Paul might be sitting on the couch watching TV, I'll take his cock out of his pants and start to massage it. He never fails to get real hard, and I always take that as a compliment. I don't expect him to do anything in return, although he often does. Sometimes I prefer it if he just sits back and enjoys it. I like to rub his cock until he shoots his sperm all over my fingers. I love it when all that sperm comes shooting out. I never saw it happen before. His cock gets all wet and slippery at the end, and then squirt, squirt, squirt, out it comes. Sometimes I keep on massaging him until he goes soft again, and my hands and his cock and his balls are all spermy all over. Other times I'll lick it off my fingers in front of him, real slow. Once I massaged it all over my face, but what really turns him on is when I unbutton my shirt and take one of my breasts out of my bra, and rub sperm around and around all over it.

"Six months ago I never could have *thought* about doing anything like that, let alone discussed it, even though I know you're not going to use my name. But I love Paul, and you're absolutely right when you say that there's nothing wrong with two people who love each other doing anything they want to turn each other on, provided they both enjoy it. In fact I think I'd go even further and say that two people who love each other have a *duty* to do everything they can to turn each other on."

The sense of release that comes with the realization that you *can* and *should* do whatever you can to maximize your sexual enjoyment is one of the most beneficial results of sexual self-training.

"I'd Never Expose Myself to My Husband"

There are still so many lovers who, when questioned, are sure that their sex life is "completely satisfying," but still have enormous inhibitions. Not through any fault of their own, but because they have never had access to any kind of practical sexual guidance.

"I wouldn't lie with my legs open and let my husband stare at my private parts, no. Why should I? They're private." That from a 34-year-old woman from Livingston, New Jersey, who had borne her husband four children with those very same "private" parts. "I wouldn't let my wife masturbate me, no. It's for men to make love to their wives, not to have them jerk them off." That from a 33-year-old man from Akron, Ohio, who had admitted buying pornography "more than once a month" and who masturbated regularly.

"What sexual training? Sex is doing what comes naturally. There's even a song about it. You put it in, you take it out." That from a 41-year-old auto mechanic from Bethlehem, Pennsylvania, married for the second time. "My mom always told me that sex was a duty which a wife had to perform for her husband. I know now, from talking to my girlfriends, that it's supposed to be a pleasure as well as a duty, but it's taken me a long time to overcome the feeling that I was brought up with, that a woman isn't supposed to enjoy it; that it's something greasy and mechanical, to do with men, like mending the sink disposal unit. I've never had an orgasm, no. At least, I'm not aware that I've ever had an orgasm. My girlfriends tell me I must, that I'm missing out on such a lot, but I really don't know how to go about it. Sometimes I feel like crying." That from a 32-year-old part-time librarian from Cleveland.

"My boss invited me out for dinner. I liked him a lot, so I accepted. At the end of the evening, we went back to his hotel room, and we kissed and undressed. He kissed my breasts, which I liked, but then he started kissing me between the legs, and trying to touch me with his tongue. He turned me over on the bed and started licking my bottom. That was more than I could stand. I got up and dressed. All the time he was yelling at me that I was a frigid cow. I'll never forget it as long as I live. I know that I'm a warm, passionate human being. I wasn't afraid to make love. But that doesn't mean that I'm prepared to take part in deviant acts." This was said by a 28-year-old secretary from Norwich, Connecticut, who had been engaged to be married three times—and each time her fiancé had called off the engagement.

A satisfying and sexual relationship—one in which both partners can reach the peak of their ability to give each other the greatest of erotic pleasure—and (just as important) to receive the greatest of erotic pleasure in return—depends more than anything else on *total intimacy*.

By *total intimacy* I mean the willing and loving exposure of your whole sexuality to each other—both your minds and bodies. In order to reach the very peak of sexual performance, *both of you* must learn to hold nothing back. If either of you has any unfulfilled desires, no matter how insignificant you may think they are, you should always share them. If either of you feels the urge to do something—or have it done to you in return—then you should learn to share that urge, too. Peak-performance sex is based on complete personal honesty, and an open, ongoing discussion. *Talk* to your partner about what you want. *Talk* to your partner about what you want him or her to do to you. And above all, *talk* to yourself about your own needs. A total lack of inhibition starts from within yourself. *Admit* that you'd love to have oral sex. *Admit* that you'd love to see the woman in your life dressed in black stockings and garter belt. *Admit* that you'd love to try sucking, licking, and touching in all of those places that other sex manuals never mention.

This is Vanessa, 19, an interior designer from Hartford, Connecticut: "When I first dated boys, I used to be very reserved about sex because I always used to get so wet when I was aroused. I would only have to kiss a boy after a date and my panties were always soaking. I used to think that there was something unpleasant about it, and for that reason I always used to shy away from any intimate contact. I wouldn't let boys put their hands up my skirt because I knew that my panties would be wet.

"It was only when I met Carl that I realized that wetness was a plus, not a minus; and that wetness actually turns men on. We met at a company party, and after the party he took me back to his apartment for coffee and—would you believe it?—opera. He had about a hundred CDs of Verdi and Puccini, and he made me the best espresso coffee I'd ever drunk, and played *Madam Butterfly*. We sat on the couch and he kissed me, and I could *feel* myself getting wetter. I was so embarrassed, I was almost ready to make some kind of excuse and leave. I didn't want him to touch me—well, not *there*, anyway.

"But he started caressing my breasts through my blouse. It was very arousing, because my blouse was silk, and the slippery feeling of it made my nipples stand up. Then he started running his hands down the sides of my thighs; and even though I *wanted* to leave, I couldn't. I needed Carl too much that evening: I wanted him to make love to me. That was the first time in my life that I thought: this is it, this is it, it's now or never.

Wet Means Willing

"He lifted up my skirt and my panties were so wet that they were almost transparent. But to my amazement, Carl didn't even notice them; or didn't seem to. He seemed to *expect* that my panties would be wet. He tugged them down, and dropped them on the floor, and he didn't say a word. I tried to keep my legs closed because I didn't want him to see me, but he opened up my thighs, gently but very strongly, and there I was, completely exposed. My pubic hair was wet, and stuck to my skin, and my whole pussy was shining with wet. I felt hot and freezing both at once, because I was so embarrassed—but do you know what he did? He kissed me on the lips; one of those lovely long lingering kisses. Then he lowered his head, and opened up my pussy with his fingers, and dipped his tongue into my pussy-hole. I actually saw him do it. I saw his tongue sliding into my pussy-hole, and then licking all around it. I saw him licking all that wetness that I was so frightened of. I saw a string of wetness clinging to the end of his tongue. I even saw him licking my pee-hole, the very tip of his tongue probing right into it; and I almost *fainted*. I didn't know feelings like this could *exist*. I didn't know that people could do things like this to each other and *live*.

"With my own eyes I actually saw him take my clitoris between his lips and tug it—very gently but firmly, and I wasn't only turned on, I was fascinated. I mean really fascinated. I suddenly understood that two people who want to excite each other in bed can do anything they want to; anything at all.

"I did things with Carl that opened my eyes to the real beauty of sex. What in the world is more beautiful than lying in bed on a sunny Sunday morning, and taking your lover's balls into your mouth? You can lick them and play with them. You can roll his cock up against your cheek. You can suck him and you can do just about anything you want. That's what I used to adore with Carl. There were no physical barriers, none whatsoever. If he had ever said to me, in the middle of the day, 'Take down your panties, I want to look at your pussy,' I would have done it. In fact, I *did* do it a couple of times, and I'd do it again with any man. Provided I had just as much freedom to look at his cock."

2

How to Bare Your All

These days, many couples find that using a video camcorder to record their lovemaking is both erotic and very helpful. You'd be surprised how much you can learn about your own sexual athleticism (or *lack* of it) by watching replays of yourself and your lover in the throes of passion.

To begin with, of course, you will probably be self-conscious about the presence of the camcorder, and have a tendency to ham it up a little. But when you become accustomed to it, it will graphically reveal to you most of those areas where you *could* be performing better. The most dramatic revelation of all is the way you *time* your lovemaking. Your sense of timing is almost always distorted when you're actually making love, and when you watch yourself on videotape you will be amazed at how long it took you to do this particular thing and how short a time it took you to do *that* particular thing. Almost without exception, men are astonished how quickly they ejaculate after first penetration. "Up until now, I really thought I was a stayer," said 29-year-old Clark, an electrician from Terre Haute, Indiana, after watching himself come to a climax in only a minute and 17 seconds after inserting his penis into his wife Pam. But Pam said, "This doesn't surprise me at all. I love him, and he's a great guy, when it always seems like he's finished before I've even warmed up." So the video analysis of Clark's performance was—for him—incontrovertible evidence that he needed to work on his timing.

Probably the best part about using a camcorder is that it's impartial. It can show a man what's wrong with his sexual performance without his lover having to pluck up the courage to tell him that he's coming too quickly, or that he's not caressing or stimulating her sufficiently, or that he's rubbing her clitoris too roughly. And *vice versa*, of course.

What makes the use of home video recordings particularly interesting is that women (who are not naturally aroused by pornographic photographs) tend to find videos not only informative but very erotic. A still photograph of a naked man can leave them absolutely cold, but to watch a moving image of a couple making love can often stimulate them intensely—even when the couple is themselves and their lover.

Here's Terri, a 23-year-old beautician from Van Nuys, California: "My boyfriend Jim made a video which he called 'A Day In the Life of Terri.' It starts off with me lying in bed, nude, pretending to be asleep, and the camera really roams all over my body. I like the opening bit, I think it's the most artistic, because my hair's spread out all over the pillow and I've got one hand on my breast, and I'm gently sort of playing with my nipple as if I'm having a sexy dream.

"Then the camera follows me into the shower and shows me washing myself all over. Then I get out of the shower and sit on the bathroom stool, and open up my legs, and tug at my pubic hair, to show that I think it's too long and that I need a bikini shave. I trim my hair with nail scissors, really tugging out my cunt-lips so that you can see everything. Then I squirt all of this shaving foam between my legs and start to shave myself. I do it real slow and sensual, sliding my fingers into my cunt so that I can stretch my cunt-lips taut, and shave them real close.

"Afterwards I rinse my bare cunt at the basin, and then go back into the bedroom. I lie back on the bed and pull my cunt wide open with my fingers so that the camera can zoom in close. That's the shot that *I* like the most. It's a real turn-on to see yourself that way. I have these real scarlet fingernails, actually the color was called Scarlet Flame, and you can see my fingers stroking and pulling my cunt-lips, and these long red fingernails dipping deep into my cunt, and then quickly flipping my clitoris. It's incredible to watch the juice starting to run out of your own cunt, and how the lips swell up. You can hear me panting all the way through this part, and how my fingers suddenly start to thrust deeper into my cunt. Near the end, I stretch my actual cunt-hole real wide, which I never realized I did, you can see right up inside me, and my fingers are flying so fast on my clitoris they're practically a blur.

"Then I climax, and you can't see much of that because I was jumping around.

"After that, you see me stepping into my thong. I pull it up real tight so that it practically disappears into my cunt, and you can see the bare lips of my cunt on either side. Then I put on my skirt and blouse and brush my hair and everything and go outside. There isn't too much outside, but there's this one great scene that Jim shot in the park. I'm sitting astride this brick wall, and you can see all the traffic and the people walking past in the background. But I lift up this little pleated skirt at the back, so that you can see my bare bottom. Jim zooms in real close, and I push my bottom out a bit, and the whole screen is filled up with the cheeks of my bottom pressed up against this rough brick wall, with the elastic of my thong real tight down the middle, and my hand reaches around and pulls the elastic to one side and I start to fondle and touch my asshole. This is a beautiful scene, real sharp and close-up, you can see everything. The sun's shining on the tiny gold hairs on my skin, my fingers keep touching and stroking my asshole, and you can see it kind of wincing like a flower, you know? I lick one of my fingers to make it slippery, then I push it up into the hole, you can see the scarlet fingernail disappearing up my ass, then two fingers, so that my asshole is stretched out. Then I'm taking out my fingers and holding the cheeks of my bottom wide apart, and gently rubbing and rotating my bare asshole against the brick wall. And all this is in sunlight, in the park, in the open air.

"Later on the video goes back to our apartment, and we put the camera on a tripod and took videos of ourselves making love. Jim comes into the bedroom, wearing just jeans, and I'm sitting on the bed, pretending to read a magazine. I keep on reading the magazine while Jim takes off his jeans. He has a huge hard-on, and he stands by the bed rubbing it up and down a few times. Then when I *still* don't take any notice, he climbs onto the bed and starts kissing my stomach and my thighs and then he runs his tongue all the way down to my cunt. This is another of my favorite scenes, because it shows Jim licking my cunt, and then I took the camera off the tripod and took some close-ups myself. You can see him sliding his tongue right into my cunt-hole, and licking my lips, and then he probes right up to my clitoris with the tip of his tongue, and there's this moment where you can see his tongue tip right underneath my clitoris, and it kind of makes my clitoris swell up.

Make Love Now,
Watch Yourself Later

"After that, there's a whole lot of us actually making love. There's this one scene where I'm lying back on the bed, and Jim's on top of me, and I'm begging him to put his cock in me. Before we made the video, we'd never done anything like this before, I guess we were acting—what do they call it?—improvising. I'm begging him and begging him. My legs are wide apart and I'm stretching open my cunt with my fingers, saying please, *please* fuck me! He keeps teasing me by just pushing the head of his cock in and then taking it out again. But at last he decides to put me out of my agony and slides his cock right in, right up to the balls. You should see that, it's fantastic, because when he slides it out again, it's all glistening with juice.

"He fucked me real slow when we were making the video because we both wanted it to last, but we realized that we were actually enjoying it more than we usually did, I mean *much* more. It was a total turn-on, the idea that we were filming ourselves and that we would be able to watch it all later. It was almost as exciting as being watched by somebody else, but still keeping it private, if you know what I mean.

"At the very end of the video, Jim lifts his cock up, and I guide him with my fingers so that he's still inside me, just, but half of the hole at the end of his cock is showing above my cunt-lips. Then he comes, and you can see the sperm flooding out of his cock, all white and thick, and pouring down between my legs."

Terri was an extrovert. She looked pretty and well-groomed and she enjoyed showing herself off to the camera. Of course, most women are much shyer, and will not be so eager to have their nudity and their lovemaking recorded on video. All the same, when it comes to sexual self-training, the benefits of seeing yourselves making love are enormous—and once you *have* taken the plunge and made one or two recordings, you will both find that many of your inhibitions about sex and your bodies have become things of the past.

If anything, the greatest inhibition that many women have about having themselves recorded on video is that they're ashamed of their bodies. "Oh my God, I didn't realize my bottom was as big as that!" exclaimed 31-year-old Candice, a sales assistant from Schaumburg, Illinois, when she saw herself naked on video for the first time. "And will you look at my breasts, they're enormous!"

Even some men are startled by their appearance on camera. Ken, a 38-year-old airport security guard, said, "That's it. Goodbye cheeseburgers, hello squash court!" In any case, television has the effect of making you look squatter and fatter than you really are. But there's no harm in taking a good long look at your body on the screen, and asking yourself whether your sexual self-training program could include a little dieting and extra exercise.

We'll discuss the further use of camcorders later, when we talk about sexual self-assessment. But there's no doubt that they're proving to be one of the most useful modern aids to better lovemaking and heightened erotic awareness. Even at times when you have no current sexual partner, you can use a camcorder to record your own responses to masturbation techniques, so that when you *do* find a partner, you'll have a clear and structured idea of what turns you on the most—and how.

You will have realized by now that you will be

learning how to reach your sexual peak through some extremely revealing firsthand discussions about intimate behavior. Many of the people who talked to me about their sexual activities were—like Terri—more sexually open and exhibitionistic than the average. Some were less self-confident, and preferred to write their experiences in diary form. But all of them were prepared to share their sexual pleasures with others, because they were proud of what they had been able to achieve, and because they wanted others to enjoy the incredible satisfaction and joy that a good sexual relationship can provide.

By reading *their* experiences, you will be able to improve your sexual expertise and your sexual athleticism within days—and because you're relying on tried-and-tested sexual acts, accompanied by expert comment, you won't have to wonder if you're doing it right or wrong.

You will be able to widen your sexual knowledge and your understanding of what you can expect out of sex. Eventually, you will be able almost to double your sexual staying power, and to double the pleasure of your climaxes. You will discover how to use everything from classic Japanese pillow-book techniques to state-of-the-art sex aids. Sexually, you will leave your old life behind, and start enjoying a thrilling, arousing, and deeply satisfying new sex life.

It doesn't matter what your present sexual relationships are like. It doesn't matter how old you are, how out of shape you are, or what personal difficulties you have. A real and noticeable and *lasting* improvement in your sex life can be yours.

3

Better Sex Takes Two

Of course, improving your sex life isn't as straightforward as improving your swimming technique or brushing up your salesmanship or learning how to service your own automobile. While accomplishments like these depend on nothing more than your own initiative, exploiting your sexual potential to the max is something that you can't do entirely by yourself.

You also have to persuade your lover to exploit his or her sexual potential to the max—and for many of us, that isn't an easy proposition. Sometimes our partner's sexual inhibitions seem to be all that's standing between us and better sex.

In fact, 67 percent of the sexually active people to whom I spoke when I was researching this book said that their sex lives could be instantly improved *if only* their partner was less inhibited/more knowledgeable/more sensitive/more attentive/or had a stronger sex drive.

Winifred, a 33-year-old dental nurse from Queens, New York, said: "I'm a very sensual person. I love making love, and if I had my way, I'd be making love all night every night. But if I start coming on to my husband, he just laughs, or goes all coy. I guess that I make him feel threatened—like I'm making all the running, and not him, and he can't stand to feel that he's not in control. But at the same time, I feel that if I *didn't* make the running, there

31

wouldn't ever *be* any running. There'd be nothing but a whole lot of standing still.''

Frank, a 26-year-old baggage handler from Los Angeles, said: "My girlfriend Cindy and I have been living together for seven months now. We make love two or three times a week, which I guess is kind of average. I love Cindy. I can genuinely and honestly say that I love her. But her attitude toward sex is very inhibited. She doesn't mind me seeing her naked . . . she's not shy in that sense. But she thinks that lovemaking is fucking, man on top of the woman, or for maximum kinks, man *beside* the woman. She won't let me touch her pussy with my fingers while we're fucking, and she certainly won't let me come within a half-mile of her ass. But I think the crunch came when she told me one evening that she'd just discovered what *Deep Throat* was all about, and she said she couldn't imagine anything dirtier or more disgusting than people doing things to each other with their *mouths*. She said, 'You wouldn't want me to do anything disgusting like that to *you*, Frank, would you?' Well . . . what's the answer to that? If I say yes she thinks I'm disgusting, if I say no I'm condeming myself to a life without blowjobs.

"I simply don't know how to handle a situation like this. I'm young, I'm fit, I *know* that sex has so much more to offer . . . but how can I make Cindy understand that sex isn't all perversion and filth?"

Educating and persuading your partner to share the pleasures of peak-performance sex will be one of the major topics of this book. You may find, indeed, that the book can speak for you. Literally thousands of readers who have bought my previous books, including *How to Drive Your Man Wild in Bed* and *How to Make Love Six Nights a Week* have written to tell me that they have found it much easier to talk about new and varied sexual acts once they have passed them along to their lover to read.

My strongest principle has always been that *nothing two lovers do together to excite and satisfy themselves sexually can be anything but beneficial to their relationship*—with the only provisos that they should never do anything physically harmful to each other, and that whatever they try must be mutually agreed-upon and mutually enjoyed.

That doesn't mean that you and your lover will necessarily enjoy each act of love equally. A man may not enjoy licking his wife's vagina as much as she enjoys having it licked. A woman may adore anal intercourse, whereas her lover finds it too strenuous and restricting. There has to be give-and-take in every sexual relationship, and there will be few times when both partners reach the highest levels of erotic stimulation at the same time. That isn't what good sex is all about, and that's certainly not what peak-performance sex is all about.

Simultaneous Orgasm: The Truth

The notion that good sex depends on you and your lover reaching simultaneous climaxes is, in my opinion, the silliest and most damaging fallacy about sex ever dreamed up by soft-core pornographers, wishful thinkers, and the writers of romantic fiction. Yet it still lingers, even today, despite the fact that—on a night-to-night basis—couples rarely have simultaneous climaxes, and even the fittest and most well-attuned couple can seldom do it to order.

The fallacy of the "simultaneous climax" leads countless women to fake their climaxes when their partner ejaculates, because they are nowhere near orgasm. This in turn leads men to believe that they have satisfied their partners when they simply haven't, and therefore they won't take the trouble to make sure that they *do* satisfy them the next time they make love. It's a vicious cycle that leads to more frustration, arguments, and sexual dissatisfaction than any other single factor.

The plain fact of the matter is that most women need more erotic stimulation than men to reach a climax—longer, slower, and more persistent. Sometimes it takes a great deal of patience (and stamina, too) for a man to bring his partner to orgasm. Said 33-year-old Mark, a draftsman from Seattle: "I diddled Susan's clitoris for five minutes . . . then ten. I was beginning to get a cramp in my arm and I thought that my diddling finger was going to drop off. I stopped but she gasped, 'Don't stop!' and so I carried on. Gradually she began to tighten her muscles and breathe quicker, but every time I thought she was close to having an orgasm she'd suddenly sigh and relax and I felt like I had to start over. At last she was really juicy and her stomach muscles were tight and she began to clench up. It must have taken all of fifteen minutes diddling . . . and if you try to diddle your finger for fifteen minutes flat you'll know how difficult that gets to be. But at last she had an orgasm, and she shook, and she shook, and she almost cried; and I kissed her and held her tight and I thought to myself, damn it, it was worth it, she's lovely."

If you're a man, how often have you taken the time and the trouble to masturbate your partner like that? If you're a woman, how many times have you encouraged the man in your life to let his fingers do the turning-on, and shown him the right way to do it?

Most sexually active people believe that sexual excellence is "essential" for a well-rounded and happy life. More than 65 percent of the people I interviewed for this book agreed that—for them—satisfying sex was a must. But at the same time only 27 percent considered their own sex life to be "consistently excellent." And of the remainder, only 13 percent "have considered, or would consider, a structured program of sexual improvement in order to reach the maximum sexual satisfaction."

In other words, we all feel that we *ought* to be better lovers, but when it comes down to the nitty-gritty, we're almost always too lazy/proud/shy/inhibited/embarrassed to take practical steps to improve our performance.

Let me explain a little more specifically what I mean by "performance." I'm certainly not talking about sex as a kind of circus act that you and your lover have to put on for each other. What I *am* talking about is a skillful and knowledgeable use of your body and an expressive use of your feelings which—when combined—will make you not only capable of *giving* tremendous sexual pleasure, but of *receiving* it, too.

It always strikes me as curious that, although most sex manuals tell you quite clearly how to stimulate and satisfy your partner ("*squeeze* his penis, titillate her clitoris"), none of them seem to recognize that it is just as important for you to know how to *receive* stimulation and satisfaction in return.

Sex is a complex intermingling of giving and taking, of activity and passivity, and knowing *when* to be active and *when* to be passive can make all the difference. Women don't always want to be the recipient of the sex act. Sometimes they feel like taking over, and doing what *they* want to do. Even though men are physically stronger, and traditionally seem to believe that the sexual initiative should

be theirs, there are times when they should be submissive and allow their partners to explore *them*.

This is Heidi, a 25-year-old secretary from Milwau-
kee: "My husband Charlie has always been very
assertive about sex. He almost always initiates our
lovemaking, and if he *doesn't* reach over and start
caressing me, then I kind of get the feeling that he
isn't in the mood, if you understand what I mean,
and so we don't make love that evening. But one
day about two or three months ago, he came home
from a business trip in California, and he went
directly to bed because he was so tired. I let him
sleep for a couple of hours, then I went into the
bedroom and took off my clothes and climbed into
bed with him. He'd been away for nearly a week
and I'd really missed him.

"I started by caressing his shoulders and his chest,
but then my hand gradually went down to his cock.
He was soft at first, but it only took three or four
strokes of my hand, and his cock began to stiffen
up. I'm not sure whether he was asleep or only half-
asleep. Whatever, he didn't open his eyes and he
didn't move, and he didn't give me any sign that
he knew what I was doing. I kept on rubbing his
cock until it was huge—then I drew back the sheets
and there it was.

"The strange thing was, that was the first time I'd
actually held his cock in my hand and really looked
at it closely. I was amazed how shiny the skin was,
on the head of it. Kind of bluish-pink, and very soft.
I stroked the opening in his cock. You don't usually
get the chance to do that, in a relationship. It was
wet with this clear, sticky lubricant, which made a
spider's-web thread when I took my finger away. I
loved the way the skin on his cock moved up and
down when I rubbed up; and his balls were all tight
and wrinkled, like walnuts. I had the opportunity

to touch him everywhere, to rub his cock up and down, just to *look* at him. I mean—how many wives really know what their husbands *look* like?'' I discovered that Charlie had a mole on the side of his cock, which I'd never noticed before.

''I kissed the head of his cock, and rubbed it from side to side against my lips. Then I sucked it gently, and pushed the tip of my tongue into the opening. I could taste the lubricant . . . I couldn't describe it, but it wasn't unpleasant. Just salty and sugary, like glucose water.

''I sucked him and rubbed him for a while . . . then I climbed on top of him, and kissed him, and guided his cock up in between my legs. I loved the sense of being in charge. I was fucking him, not him fucking me, and I was going up and down on his cock like Calamity Jane on her favorite horse.

''I guess he hadn't been deeply asleep, but now he woke up and smiled at me, and said, 'What are you doing?' and *I* said, 'I'm making *love* to you, that's what I'm doing.' So immediately he tried to push me over so that he was on top of me, but I leaned forward and kissed him and said, 'No, it's my turn.' And he had to stay on his back while I rode up and down on him.

''I don't think he liked it all that much . . . not that first time. He felt helpless. He didn't like me sitting on top of him like that. But *I* liked it, because if I sat up straight his cock went deep up inside me; but if I leaned forward it rubbed against the sides of my cunt in such a fantastic way. I suddenly found that I was in charge of the feelings I got, and I fucked and rubbed and fucked and rubbed until suddenly I knew that I was going to have an orgasm.

''It was like somebody tipped a whole bucketful of warm water all over me. It was so wonderful, I thought I was going to lose my mind. I leaned forward and I hugged Charlie tight, and he pushed his cock up me five or six times, quite hard, and I heard him breathing in my ear; and then *he* came too. I felt him come, which was something that I'd never felt before. I actually felt the sperm coming out of him; and that gave me another shiver, kind of a mini-orgasm; and then another, and another.

Women on Top

"Afterwards we lay side by side and didn't say anything for a long time. We didn't have to. But I think we'd both learned something. Charlie had learned that I *could* take charge, when it came to making love, and that sometimes he was going to find himself making love to me when he didn't really want to . . . the same way thousands of women all over the world must find every damned night that their husbands or lovers are making love to *them* when they don't really want to.

"Like you said, it's give and take. I'd learned to give and Charlie had learned to take. Just a little. He still prefers to be in charge. But when I feel like making love, believe me, I make love, and there's nothing that Charlie can do to stop me."

So—let's ask ourselves what we really want out of our sex lives. We want more than anything else to show our partners that we love them, and that they excite us. We want physical and emotional stimulation. We want satisfaction, which may not necessarily mean that either of us has to have a climax, and which certainly doesn't mean that we have to have a simultaneous climax.

We want to feel refreshed; we want to feel closer. Your age and your physical condition don't matter. When we talk about peak-performance sex we're not talking about world records. We're talking about achieving the very best of which you're capable—pushing yourself to the limits of your own ability. If you follow this guide, you *can* and *will* do better. At times, you'll amaze yourself, I promise.

All you have to do is assess yourself as realistically and as honestly as you can; and then set yourself a series of *achievable* sexual goals.

Before we start our exploration of peak-performance sex, however, a totally serious word to the wise:

It has always been good sexual practice for lovers to observe basic hygiene and to ensure that their partners are not suffering from any kind of venereal infection, such as non-specific urethritis, gonorrhea, or genital herpes.

These days, it is also essential to protect yourself against the possibility of contracting AIDS. I want you to give your peak performance, not your final performance.

You should therefore practice safe sex. Groups at high risk for exposure to the AIDS virus include intravenous drug users, homosexual and bisexual men, and prostitutes. All the same, limiting your sexual partners is no absolute guarantee. Unless you are certain *beyond any doubt* that your lover is not carrying AIDS, you should:

Always wear a condom when making love, and always make sure that the man's penis is completely removed from the vagina before the condom is taken off.

Avoid oral sex, and never swallow semen or urine. AIDS is passed on by the exchange of bodily fluids, and by blood and semen in particular.

Avoid unprotected anal intercourse. Rectal tissues

can often be slightly torn during anal sex, opening your body to infection.

These days, even the raunchiest of porno stars are insisting on HIV tests before they will think of participating in on-screen sex. These are professionals—you would be very wise to follow their example.

In this book, you will find numerous descriptions of oral and anal sex. After all, they are thrilling, satisfying and highly intimate sexual activities, and to omit them from a guide to exciting sex would be absurd.

But I have to caution you against any act of intercourse without a condom, and especially against oral and anal sex, unless your partner has undergone an AIDS test. All of the sexual acts discussed in this book should be regarded as subject to this essential stricture.

Another—less doomy—word of caution: this book will take you to the cutting edge of modern sexual knowledge and experience. I am assuming that—if you go farther—you are prepared to read about erotic practices which—five or ten years ago—were considered too bizarre or unusual to include in a mainstream sexual guide.

Ten years ago, for example, it would have been unthinkable for a sex-aid manual to advertise specially shaped vibrators that were openly designed for "high-speed anal stimulation" . . . or the "Jelly Baby Softy Bully Boy Dildo . . . made in the latest super, slippy, sloppy, slimy, sensuous jelly substance developed in Japan." Five years ago, only "encyclopedias of sex" discussed the erotic excitement of rubber, or bondage, or mild acts of sadomasochism, or erotic clothing, or pubic shaving, or wet sex.

But to reach the peak of your sexual performance, you will have to set aside all of your reservations and all of your inhibitions, and really let yourself go. The experience will be breathtaking, exciting, and sometimes alarming. You will have to take risks with yourself, and with your partner, too. At the end of the day, however, you should be able to acknowledge that you are a much better lover; and that your partner is a much better lover, too; and that between you, you have reached heights of sexual pleasure that you simply couldn't imagine.

This is Alexandra, 23, from Charleston, South Carolina, describing the moment when she first realized that her sexual enjoyment didn't need to be limited by convention or upbringing or "what was considered decent."

"I'm afraid it took a few glasses of champagne to liberate me. I'd gone to a pretty stuffy barbecue with my boyfriend Peter. It was something to do with his legal work, and I was supposed to look pretty and behave myself. The trouble was, I hadn't had anything to eat all day, and I didn't have much of an appetite for semi-raw lumps of meat; so I ended up drinking a whole bottle of champagne *at least* on an empty stomach, and by the time that eleven o'clock came I was being giggly and stupid and almost falling over.

"Peter drove me back to my apartment and laid me on the bed. I asked him to make love to me but he wouldn't, he said I needed coffee more than I needed sex. I undressed because at least I was sober enough to take care of my dress. Then I lay back on the bed naked and closed my eyes and waited for Peter.

"My hand strayed down between my legs and I started to masturbate. I don't really know why. I don't masturbate very often, although I used to do it quite a lot when I was younger. I suppose I was drunk, that's all, and felt horny. Anyway, it got to the point where I was furiously rubbing myself, with my legs wide open, and Peter walked in with two mugs of coffee.

"He didn't know what to do. But I said, 'Stay, stay, sit down, I'm nearly finished.' It gave me a thrill, letting him see that I masturbated—and, after all, he made love to me, he stuck his cock in me, he'd seen me naked enough times—what was the difference? I kept on rubbing myself and he sat down on the corner of the bed and watched me. He didn't say anything. I don't know what he felt. He just watched me.

"I was almost there when I began to feel a pain in my bladder. I really needed a pee. I should have got up, but I was drunk enough to think 'what the hell, he's seen everything, he can see this.' I lifted my legs up and I peed in the air, a long hot stream of it, and it splashed all over my face and all over my breasts and all over my stomach. I was all wet and warm and smelling of pee, and I massaged my breasts and my nipples and went on masturbating myself until I came. I had such a climax I felt like I was cracking in half; and before I was even finished, Peter had pulled off his tuxedo pants and was right on top of me, fucking me hard. We had the fiercest, deepest kiss you could ever imagine, and I had another climax, and then Peter climaxed, too, and then we lay side by side on the bed just staring at each other. Do you know what Peter said? He said, 'We just went through a something-barrier. I'm not sure what kind of barrier, but it was a something-barrier. A sex barrier, an embarrassment barrier, I don't know.'

"These days, we're close like *this* [crossing her fingers]. I think we discovered that day that we're just people, you know? He's a man, and I'm a woman, and we love each other. Why hide anything; why not do whatever you want to do? And I mean whatever.''

Alexandra is typical of many young men and women today. Unlike the young people of the 1960s, their sexual experiences aren't promiscuous or casual or nondiscriminatory. They're mature and liberated enough to form lasting and wide-ranging relationships, and within those relationships, to strive to reach the High Sierras of sexual pleasure.

You can be up there with them.

4

Test Your Sexual Performance

Here is a quick checklist of your sexual attitudes and sexual achievements. It is designed to help you to assess your sexual performance and judge for yourself which special areas of your sex life need to be improved. Answer as honestly as you can, because the more truthful you are, the more accurate your assessment will be. From an accurate assessment, you will be able to improve your sexual capabilities much more quickly and effectively.

1. Most of the time, I am easily sexually stimulated   Yes/No
2. I am often too tired for lovemaking   Yes/No
3. I always enjoy sex   Yes/No
4. I do not think I make love often enough Yes/No
5. I enjoy exposing myself sexually to my partner   Yes/No
6. I do not like making love with the lights on   Yes/No
7. I am prepared to try any sexual act   Yes/No
8. I do not know very much about sex   Yes/No
9. I would like to find out more about different sexual acts   Yes/No
10. I would never consider masturbating in front of my partner   Yes/No

11. I have frequently indulged in oral sex
    Yes/No

12. I think that sex should be confined to the bedroom   Yes/No

13. I have told my partner my most secret erotic thoughts   Yes/No

14. I would never use vibrators or other sex toys
    Yes/No

15. I have told my partner what stimulates me the most   Yes/No

16. I have faked a climax more than once
    Yes/No

17. I frequently try to have sex more than once a night   Yes/No

18. I find it hard to keep my concentration during sex   Yes/No

19. I enjoy casual sexual touching during the day
    Yes/No

20. I think sex magazines and videos are repulsive   Yes/No

21. I get completely involved in lovemaking
    Yes/No

22. I think that the importance of sex is overrated   Yes/No

23. I would dress up in erotic clothing to stimulate my partner   Yes/No

24. I think some sexual acts are dirty   Yes/No

25. I think that better sex is one important reason to keep fit   Yes/No

26. I do not think that I am a particularly outstanding lover   Yes/No

27. I always try to find out what my partner's sexual needs are   Yes/No

28. I think my partner is completely satisfied sexually   Yes/No

29. I always try to make sure that my partner climaxes   Yes/No

30. I do not like my partner touching me anally Yes/No

31. I enjoy kissing and caressing my partner whether we make love or not   Yes/No

32. I expect my interest in sex to decline as I get older   Yes/No

33. It still excites me to see my partner naked   Yes/No

34. My partner's sexual demands sometimes seem too extreme   Yes/No

35. I would be interested in improving my sexual performance   Yes/No

36. I would never let my partner make sex videos of me   Yes/No

37. I would like to achieve a more intensive climax   Yes/No

Score 3 points for every *even-numbered* question to which you answered Yes and deduct 3 points for every *even-numbered* question to which you answered No. Deduct 3 points for every *odd-numbered* question to which you answered Yes and score 3 points for every *odd-numbered* question to which you answered No.

There is a possible maximum score of 108. If you scored between 93 and 108, you are a highly sexually motivated individual who recognizes not only the importance of your own sexual needs but also the sexual needs of your partner. You are generous and giving when it comes to sex, because you know that by *giving* pleasure, you will receive pleasure in return. You do not flinch from sexual experimentation, and you have a healthy respect for your own body. You are open-minded about new sexual experiences, although you have a tendency to think that your sex life is so good that it does not require any major improvement.

If you scored between 72 and 93, you are an unusually caring and daring lover, and you enjoy sex wholeheartedly. You do not always concentrate fully on your lovemaking, however, because you allow domestic or professional anxieties to interfere instead of thinking only of sexual pleasure—both for you and for your partner. You have a positive attitude about the role of sexual satisfaction in your life, but you are not as adventurous as you might be. You would be prepared to listen to advice about improving your sexual pleasure, but you would be likely to select only those activities and exercises that did not embarrass you or go against your preconceived ideas about what is and is not sexually acceptable.

If you scored between 54 and 72, you understand that sex is a critical part of your life, but you are lacking in sexual knowledge and sexual self-confidence—not necessarily through any fault of your own. You are inhibited by the feeling that sex is an activity that should be performed only in bed and only at bedtime and not freely discussed at any other time. You have strong sexual fantasies but you are often afraid to express them to your partner, fearing that he or she may consider them offensive or upsetting. Although you derive a good deal of satisfaction from your lovemaking, you tend not to criticize your partner or to show him or her how to stimulate you more intensely. There have been many occasions when you have gone without a climax or simulated one.

If you scored between 33 and 54, you have strong inhibitions about sex that you should consider as carefully and as self-analytically as possible. Did your parents have a very restrictive attitude about sex? Was your first introduction to lovemaking painful or awkward or embarrassing? Did you have an unhappy sexual relationship? Do personal or family problems make it hard for you to concentrate on your sexual satisfaction and well-being? Do you have sexual difficulties, such as climaxing too soon (if you're a man) or failing to reach orgasm (if you're a woman)? Whatever it is, don't despair. Sexual problems, because of the physical and emotional tensions involved, almost always seem worse to the sufferer than they really are. Later on, we'll see how you can analyze your sexual problems without the need for expensive or misleading professional assistance, and how you can quickly and easily overcome some sexual problems that you thought were insurmountable.

If you scored lower than 33, you may need to talk to a professional counselor about your sexual reserve. But although I have seen many people with serious sexual dysfunctions, I have found that those who show an interest in improving their sex lives have already taken the first step, and by reading this book, that is exactly what you have managed to do. You will need to take a metaphorical deep breath, relax, and then work calmly and systematically on adjusting your feelings about love and sex. Sex is a pleasure. Sex is a joy. Sex is a source of satisfaction and excitement. There is nothing that you can do with your partner that is wrong or degrading if both of you enjoy it.

Here's part of a letter I received from 23-year-old Iris, a canine beautician from Chicago: "We'd just come back from the market, and Brad and I were putting away the groceries. Suddenly he said, 'Look at this, sweetheart.' I looked around and he was holding a huge cucumber in front of his pants, so that it looked like a huge green cock. I laughed and told him not to act so dirty. But he said, 'You know you love it,' and he chased me around the kitchen with it. I ran around the kitchen table a couple of times, and then out into the living room.

"Brad followed me and football-tackled me onto the couch. I was struggling but he pulled up my skirt and dragged down my pantyhose, and the next thing I knew he was opening my pussy with his fingers, and pushing that massive green cucumber up me.

"I could have been angry, I guess. But I wasn't angry. Brad's always considerate and fun, and this was a sex game, that was all. That's the funny part about it. If you love the person, and you know they have nothing but love and fun in their hearts, then all you have to do is join in. I lifted my legs up and spread them wide, and kept on panting, 'Fuck me, Mr. Spock, fuck me.' And Brad kept pushing that big knobby green cucumber in and out of my pussy, until it began to make a sucking noise because I was getting so juicy. I was *enjoying* it. It was a turn-on. And why not? If you could have seen that great big green shiny thing sliding in and out of my pink pussy, I think you would have been turned on too.

"In the end Brad got jealous of the cucumber and unbuckled his pants and started to fuck me himself. Green cock, red cock. I had a climax almost instantly, one of those shivery ones that goes on and on. It was fantastic, it really was . . . and all because I hadn't allowed myself to get all crazy and upset about being fucked by a cucumber. I don't care *what* Brad does to me . . . because he loves me so much, and he's always so full of passion. In any case, nothing could persuade me to turn vegetarian, at least when it comes to sex."

5

Sex to the Max

It's often said that youth is wasted on the young, and in some ways that applies to sex more than any other activity. In our teenage years, our bodies are light and supple, our energy is almost boundless, our looks are fresh, our hormones are speeding at full throttle. Young boys can get instant and "unputdownable" erections just by *thinking* about breasts; and young girls can find their panties soaking wet after not much more than a goodnight kiss.

Only trouble is: teenage lovers are clumsy and ignorant and desperately lacking in self-confidence. Our heads are crammed with half-remembered biology lessons and schoolyard myths, and our lovemaking is guided more by superstition and spontaneity than it is by skill and expertise. It's not surprising that our first encounters of a sexual nature are often disappointing and difficult. Often, they can color our attitude toward lovemaking forever.

Teenage sex is often portrayed on television and in the movies as a subject for amusement and embarrassment. Well, yes, there isn't a boy alive who can't remember the time when he couldn't get up from the dinner table because his pants were tentpoled by a sudden and uncontrollable erection. And there are very few girls who don't still blush when they remember how wet they were when a boy first touched them *there*.

The serious side to teenage sex, however, is that those early experiences color and affect our sexual attitudes for the rest of our lives—sometimes with positive results, but more often with inhibiting results. Our parents may tell us that babies aren't generally found under gooseberry bushes, and our teachers may tell us something about the details of human biology and even something about sexual relationships. But who tells us about the *skills* of sex? And, more important, what degree of pleasure and satisfaction we can expect from our sexual encounters?

Because of this, most young people—at the very peak of their physical sexuality—have awkward and unsatisfying sexual relationships, and expect very little from sex, sometimes for the rest of their lives.

This is Noreen, 47 years old, a homemaker from Paterson, New Jersey: "I married the second boy I ever slept with. His name was Eric and I'd always had a crush on him at school. He was captain of the basketball team and he was very handsome. We were married when I was 19 years old and I thought that my life was going to be some kind of dream. Well, it didn't turn out that way at all. The trouble was that both of us were very inexperienced when it came to lovemaking . . . in fact, Eric was just as inexperienced as I was, in spite of the fact that he'd dated scores of girls. His idea of making love was to fumble around with my breasts for a while, then climb on top of me and push himself in, whether I was ready or not. He'd grunt and strain until he came, and then roll off me and light a cigarette. Most of the time I hadn't even had the chance to *start* getting aroused.

"The result was that I was sexually frustrated for over twenty years, and that made me bad-tempered, depressed, a really terrible person. I lost all of my respect for myself and I simply didn't know why. I had to take sleeping pills. I was always argumentative and fractious. I was so unhappy I thought about leaving Eric and going to live all on my own someplace, where nobody knew me. I thought that he didn't deserve such an awful nagging wife.

"It didn't occur to me that I wasn't expecting enough out of my sex life and that he wasn't giving me what I needed. It just didn't occur to me. All of my friends said how lucky I was that I was married to such a handsome man. They'd swoon over him, and flirt with him . . . and the more they did that, the more I thought that everything that was wrong with our marriage was *my* fault, and not his.

"I didn't live in what you might call a very intellectual community. My women friends seemed to be mostly satisfied with cooking and cleaning and bringing up babies. We did talk about sex occasionally, but mostly in the context of having babies and painful periods. As far as most of my women friends were concerned, sex was just another chore, like cleaning the kitchen floor. There wasn't much in the way of consciousness-raising going on, I can tell you.

"My mother had never talked to me about sex, except to tell me how babies were conceived, and that I should always put toilet paper on the seats of public johns. She never once mentioned that it was supposed to be exciting and pleasurable, and that it was a way of expressing how much you loved your husband.

"Of course I read romantic books, but in those days they didn't exactly cross the t's and dot the i's when it came to sex. They talked a lot about crashing waves and fireworks and storms in their bosoms, but that was as far as they went.

"Orgasm After Orgasm"

"I didn't understand about orgasms at all. I'd never had one. I asked one of my friends what they were, but she got real embarrassed and said that they were just something you had when you made love. Then I read an article about them in a copy of *Cosmopolitan*, but the writer seemed to assume that everybody who was reading the article already knew what they were, so I didn't learn very much, except that every woman had the right to have them.

"Looking back now on those twenty years of marriage, I suppose it seems pathetic and ridiculous that I didn't know what an orgasm was. But I had been brought up to think that your husband knew all there was to know about sex, and because Eric seemed to be satisfied with what we were doing, it didn't occur to me to challenge his sexual competence. I was keeping my husband happy, after all, and isn't that wives are supposed to do?

"The turning point came when I met Susan, an old school friend of mine. She'd always been the dashing, daring one. She'd gotten married when she was just out of school, like I had, but then she'd left her husband and moved to California. We had lunch together and she told me all about her new boyfriend, who was a dance instructor, and she said that he was so terrific in bed that he gave her 'orgasm after orgasm'—those were her exact words.

"That was how the conversation got around to orgasms. In the end, I told her that I didn't really understand what an orgasm was. At first she thought that I'd had them, but didn't know what they were called. But after a couple more glasses of wine, I relaxed enough to tell her what my sex life was really like, and she was *horrified*. She explained what an orgasm was, what it felt like—and how *necessary* it was to have one . . . maybe not every single time, but often enough to release my sexual tension.

"I have to tell you, I cried. I literally cried. When I thought of all of those years of my life, all of my youth . . . and I'd never once experienced the real joy of sex. It was like finding out after twenty years that there was something called music.

"Susan was incredibly helpful and kind. She told me how I could give *myself* a climax, you know, by masturbation. I'd never touched myself like that, and she shocked me at first, but she told me that it was perfectly normal and that millions of women masturbated regularly. Then she told me that I should tell Eric to slow down when he made love to me, and how I had a right to some foreplay, you know, to get me fully aroused before he put himself inside me. She even promised to mail me a vibrator, in case I needed a little help. She sent me a couple of books, too—including *How to Drive Your Man Wild in Bed*.

"That afternoon I went home early, and I went into the bedroom and undressed in front of the closet mirrors. I was alone, and I knew that I wasn't going to be interrupted, but I felt so nervous and ashamed! But I put some soft music on the CD player, and I rubbed a little of my favorite skin oil on my hands, and I knelt down in front of the mirror and started to massage my breasts and play with my nipples. I really took my time, and I really made myself relax. I kept remembering what Susan had said to me . . . 'you're a woman, it's your *right* that the man in your life makes love to you really well. It's your *right* to enjoy your own body.'

"I massaged my breasts until they were all red and flushed, and I teased my nipples until they stuck out hard. Then I slid my hands down my sides and my stomach, and massaged my thighs. Then I reached down between my legs, and began to stroke my pussy.

"As I say, I'd never touched myself down there before, only to wash myself, or to put in a tampon. Not like that, not to turn myself on. I felt all hot and embarrassed and strange. But the feeling was good, and I began to stroke myself more strongly. It was the same tingling feeling I got when Eric was making love to me, but much more intense—twenty times more intense than when *he* did it. Soon I had my left hand down between my thighs, and two fingers stuck right up inside my vagina, pulling and massaging, and my right hand quickly rubbing my clitoris.

"A feeling was growing inside of me that I simply couldn't believe. The funny part about it was, I wanted Eric, I wanted his cock up inside me, I wanted that more than anything . . . even though Eric had never been able to giving me a feeling like this. I imagined his cock pushing in and out of me, and I forced almost my whole hand up inside my vagina. I was so wet with pussy-juice that I couldn't believe it . . . I'd never been wet like that before. My fingers were actually making a *shlupp-schlupp-shlupp* noise as I masturbated.

"Then it happened. My whole pussy felt as if it was getting tighter and tighter, and I squeezed my eyes shut. I had an orgasm that shook me like an earthquake. I just shook and shook as if I was a rag doll and some child was shaking me. When I opened my eyes, I honestly didn't know where I was for a second, or what had happened to me. Then I saw myself kneeling naked in the mirror. My hair was stuck to my forehead with perspiration, and my chest was flushed crimson.

"I ran a bath and sat in it for a long time. Then,

really slowly, with soapy fingers, I masturbated again, and I had another orgasm. I felt as if I discovered the secret of the universe, you know? And, in a funny sort of way, I guess I had.

"The effect on Eric wasn't very good. He'd gotten set in his ways, and I don't think he liked the idea of a wife who was too pushy in bed. Apart from that—although he was good-looking, I don't think he was a particularly sexual person. He didn't like to kiss and caress and all that stuff. To him, sex was just another appetite. You're hungry, you eat a hot dog. You feel a twitch in your cock, you fuck. We stayed together for about six or seven months more, but then I left him. Not for another man—not to begin with, but to study music in New York. It wasn't too bad a separation . . . we're still friends and we still occasionally see each other. These days, I'm married to a very loving and sensitive guy who knows how to please me in bed. Unlike Eric, he can't put up a shelf, and what he knows about basketball wouldn't cover the back of a postage stamp, but he knows how to please me in bed, and that's what matters to me.

"I made a point of learning everything I could about sex and lovemaking. To me, it's more important to know how to make love than it is to know how to cook, or how to drive, or how to add two and two so that they come to four. I was so ignorant and so naive that I missed out on years and years of pleasure and satisfaction . . . and a whole lot more than that, on well-being, too. Who knows what I might have achieved in my life if I'd felt better about myself? Yet nobody told me. Not my parents, not my teachers, nobody. I dread to think how many women there are who never or scarcely ever have orgasms . . . who never even have sex that excites them or makes them feel good."

Noreen's unhappy experience is shared by countless women not only of her own generation but of today's generation of teenagers, too. Young people are still woefully ignorant about the skills of sex, not through any fault of their own, but because their parents and teachers are simply not telling them what they need to know—either because they're embarrassed, or because they feel that too much sexual knowledge will incite young people to acts of masturbation and fornication, or because they're ignorant of the skills of sex themselves—which, unfortunately, is often the reason why sex training is so inadequate.

I say "training" rather than "education" because sex is such a complex combination of physical and emotional responses that it is learned much more effectively through a structured system of practical experience than it is through theory and classroom-style lectures. In all of my books, I have described ways in which (as you acquire more sexual knowledge) you can try it out. Although it's obviously helpful to have a current sexual partner, you can still reach an advanced stage of sexual skill on your own, through varying forms of self-stimulation and exercise.

An interesting and provocative example of how a teenage girl was sexually trained came from 22-year-old Kelly, a dancer from Santa Barbara, California.

When she was 16, Kelly's parents split up, and she and her mother Kay moved to a smaller apartment in Montecito. Both Kelly and her mother are blonde and strikingly pretty—and, as Kelly said, "We've always been real close . . . because I'm an only child, and because my father was away a whole lot, Kay and me were always more like sisters than mother and daughter. We never had any secrets, and I think because of that I was able to help Kay when she and my father split up.

"As far as sex is concerned, Kay has always been totally open. She told me everything I needed to know about sex right from the moment I was old enough to understand, so when I had my first period, for example, it didn't come as any kind of a shock, like it did to some of the girls I knew. She didn't just explain about babies, she told me that sex was terrific, too, and that when I met a boy I really loved, I'd have the best time ever.

"She Usually Masturbated . . . Why Hide It?"

"She was never immoral about sex, though, or promiscuous. She always emphasized how important it was for me to find the right guy, and she herself never slept with dozens of men, although some of the local gossips tried to make out that she did. They were just jealous, I guess, and they didn't have anything better to do than bring us down. Men usually adore us, but their womenfolk don't usually take too kindly to us, but I suppose that's the price you've got to pay for being extra-attractive! [*laughs*] Kay has this wonderful bubbly personality, and she's stunning to look at. She's an inch shorter than I am, but we have exactly the same blue eyes, and the same measurements, 38-25-36, so that we can share the same clothes and everything.

"The time we got sexually the closest was when we first moved to Montecito. I was growing up and Kay was feeling lonesome, and we were really good for each other. We went swimming together, went out together, did my homework together, and we shared the same bed.

"Physically we were never shy with each other. We used to shower together, and Kay would soap me down and I'd soap her. I loved her, I *still* love her, and I don't think there's anything wrong in a girl feeling affectionate toward her own mother.

"Kay always believed that a woman should be perfectly groomed, and she used to give me manicures and pedicures and show me how to make up my eyes and how to do my hair. She'd wax my legs and shave my pubic hair for me, too . . . she did that ever since it first started to grow.

"The first night we slept together in our new apartment, she said I was going to have to get used to the idea that, before she went to sleep, she usually masturbated. She'd thought about keeping it a secret from me, but then she thought that she'd always been totally open and honest about everything else . . . why hide something which she thought was natural and normal and which she *needed* to do since she didn't have a steady man, and didn't want to go out and cruise the singles scene just because she was feeling sexually frustrated?

"I didn't mind her masturbating. In fact that first night I felt privileged in a way that she was sharing something so intimate with me. To tell you the truth, I found it exciting, too. We both slept in nightshirts, but soon after we switched out the light she lifted her nightshirt and I could feel the bed moving as she rubbed herself. She started to pant, too.

"I put my arm around her, because I kind of wanted to join in. She stopped, and switched on the light. She looked real hot, but real pretty, too. She said, 'Why don't we do it together? I'll show you how.'

"We took off our nightshirts. She kissed me, my

cheeks and then my lips, and then she fondled my breasts. She said, 'If there's one thing you inherited from me, it's your beautiful big breasts.' She kissed and sucked my nipples, and I thought how amazing it was to have your own mother sucking your nipples. She cupped her breasts in her hand, and pushed them up against my breasts, so that our nipples rubbed together. We squeezed and massaged our breasts together, and I was beginning to get really aroused. It was the first time that anybody had fondled my breasts like that, so openly. A couple of guys had got their hands into my bra, but that was about it. And to have another woman's breasts rubbing against my own was such a turn-on, particularly since it was Kay, my own mother, and not some strange lesbian.

"I've wondered a couple of times if there was anything lesbian in what we were doing, but I know that I like men too much. I like Kay too much. She wasn't seducing me, or doing anything she shouldn't. She wasn't corrupting me. In fact, she was doing the opposite. She was showing me how exciting sex could be without my having to go off and sleep with some guy that I didn't even love.

"She took a small hand-mirror and she held it between my legs. Then she opened up the lips of my vagina with her fingers, and angled the mirror so that the reflected light from the bedside lamp shone right up inside me. She showed me what the inside of my vagina looked like, and the hole where I pee from right above it, and my clitoris. She guided my hand down to touch my clitoris, and showed me the way she preferred to rub it when she masturbated, with the tip of her middle finger right on the peak of the clitoris itself, and the index finger stroking the shaft. She showed me how I could use my other fingers to tug my vaginal lips . . . which is what a man's penis does when he plunges in and out of you.

"I started to masturbate myself, but I was very tense and self-conscious. So Kay told me lie back and relax, and she did it for me. I can remember it even now. I thought it was heaven. She had such light, quick fingers . . . but she didn't hurry. She gently built me up through one layer of feeling after another, until I suddenly felt as if I had been caught up in this huge warm silent explosion. That was the night I really began to discover what sexual pleasure was all about.

"Afterwards, Kay masturbated herself, quite openly, lying on the bed in front of me with her legs apart. She inserted two fingers into her vagina while she masturbated, and tugged on her vaginal lips with her thumb. She said that practically everybody has a different way of masturbating. She knew plenty of women who could have an orgasm just by lying on their sides and squeezing their thighs together.

"For two or three months, we masturbated together almost every night. It was something I really looked forward to. I was never ashamed of it, and I never thought for a moment that it was anything but innocent fun. But it taught me a lot, too, especially about my own body. I mean you *can* train yourself to be better at sex. Kay showed me how to do things that I'd never even dreamed about. One night she opened her beside drawer and took out two vibrators. One was really thick, like a man's cock, all covered in veins. The other was very slim. I was lying naked on my stomach on the bed, reading a magazine. Kay asked me if I wanted to try out the vibrators. She said I didn't have to if I didn't want to, but *she* was. I asked her to show me first. So she lay back and opened up her thighs, and slid the big cocklike vibrator into her vagina. It was nearly ten inches long, but she managed to get most of it in. Then she switched it on, so that it started to buzz inside her. I could see her vaginal lips vibrating. After a moment or two, she took out the big vibrator and slipped the thin vibrator into her vagina, just to lubricate it. It came out all shiny with juice. Immediately she reached underneath her bottom and slid the thin vibrator into her bottom-hole, as far as it would go—then she switched that on, too. She pushed the big vibrator back into her vagina, and slowly churned it around in a circular motion. At the same time she rubbed her clitoris with her other hand.

"She started to gasp, and twist around, and say 'fuck me, fuck me,' over and over.

"I'd seen her have orgasms before, but not an orgasm like this one. It happened so quickly, and when she came her nipples stood up like buttons and her hips heaved. She screamed, and she squeezed her muscles so violently that the thin vibrator was pushed out of her bottom-hole onto the bed.

"I think I was kind of frightened of trying the vibrators at first, because Kay's orgasm had been so wild. Also I'd never thought about putting anything up my bottom-hole. I guess I thought it was dirty. But Kay said I ought to try . . . so she went to the bathroom to wash the vibrators. While I was waiting for her I lay on the bed and gently diddled myself, to get myself in the mood. But I was still frightened. Kay came back and knelt beside me on the bed. She said, 'Do you want to do this, or shall I?' I said I'd prefer it if *she* did.

"She switched on the vibrator and massaged my breasts with it. It looked so much like a real cock it was unbelievable, except that it was buzzing! It gave me a really wild tingling feeling in my nipples. They went totally hard and tight, and still Kay kept on vibrating them with this pink plastic cock, until I could hardly bear it any longer. Then she reached down and opened up my vagina and slowly worked the vibrator up me. I'd never experienced a vibrator before, and this one was just a little bigger than a real cock, so that it stretched me as well as vibrating me. Kay took hold of my hand and guided it down so that I could hold the base of the vibrator myself, and caress my own vaginal lips with my fingertips. It was an incredible sensation, being able to control this huge plastic cock right up inside me . . . I could revolve it around and around the neck of my womb, push it forward or backward, whatever I wanted. Now I began to understand why Kay had reached an orgasm so quickly.

"Now Kay slid the thin vibrator into her own vagina, to lubricate it. I could feel it touching my bottom-hole and I guess I squeezed my muscles tight, because Kay said, 'You have to relax, honey. You have to push gently against it, open your muscles up. Good lovemaking is all about muscle control.' She tried again but still my muscles tightened. I was beginning to think I wasn't going to be able to do it. Maybe I didn't really *want* to do it.

"But Kay sucked two fingers. She worked one of them up into my bottom-hole, and then the other, and stretched my bottom-hole open. For some reason, the fact that it was Kay's fingers up inside me, instead of a plastic thing, made me more relaxed. She was my mother and I trusted her completely.

"When she had stretched my bottom-hole open as wide as she could, she slid the vibrator up it, too, as far as it would go, and then switched it on. She took out her fingers, took hold of my other hand and gave me the end of the thin vibrator to hold, just like the other one.

"I think I got to Planet Nine that evening. You know they talk about the earth moving, well this was it. I started having these small rippling orgasms that wouldn't stop, they went on and on and on. Then I had a huge orgasm that felt as if I was being torn apart, then more small rippling ones, then another big one—not quite as big as the first, but big enough. And still the vibrators went on vibrating, and my muscles kept on shuddering and shaking.

"When I finally took that big cock out of me, the bed was soaking. I took the thin vibrator out carefully because my bottom-hole was sore, but Kay said that—with practice—I would soon get used to anal sex. To show me what she could take without any discomfort at all, she took the big vibrator, which was still slippery with *my* juice, lifted both legs in the air, and pushed it right up to the hilt into her bottom, seven inches long and two inches thick.

"She Can Literally Milk Him"

"She showed me that if a girl exercises her vaginal and anal muscles regularly, using anything from a carrot to a candle to a ball point pen to a thick vibrator, she can get terrific control over her lovemaking. She can get hold of a man's cock in the middle of making love and squeeze it with her vaginal muscles so tight and so rhythmically that she literally milks the sperm out of him. She can do the same with her bottom.

"I never told any of my friends what I did with my mother because they wouldn't have understood. A lot of them would have been really shocked. But

I still look back on those evenings as some of the best times I ever had with her. They were very sexy, yes, and I can understand that very few girls have that kind of free physical relationship with their mothers. But Kay taught me so much; and plenty of mothers could teach their daughters almost as much, even if they didn't want to be so physically intimate with them.

"How many mothers discuss with their daughters the kind of men they should go for and the ones they should steer well clear of? I mean, really discuss it as an issue, the way Kay and I used to. How many mothers discuss sex with their daughters, to the point where they know all of their anatomy and what it does? How many mothers tell their daughters that most men adore the taste and smell of their vaginal juice, and love to lick them between the legs? I mean, how many, truthfully?

"How many mothers tell their daughters how to masturbate, how to exercise themselves sexually, how to give a man a good time? How many mothers tell their daughters that it's even *possible* for your lover to stick his cock up your bottom, and that you might even enjoy it? How many mothers discuss orgasms and how to make them better? How many mothers talk about giving a man head, and whether you ought to swallow it or not?"

"I think Kay was a mother in a million. I mean she was really exceptional and I wouldn't expect other girls to go to bed with their mothers and masturbate together. I guess she was pretty sex-starved round about that time in her life, too. She's living with a man now, a really good man, and she's all bright-eyed and bushy-tailed, and truly happy. And I've been married for four months and my sex life is truly satisfying and good. It'll be even better when

I've finished training my husband to be as good as me."

Although it's unlikely that many mothers would consider having such an explicit sexual relationship with their daughters—or that many fathers would consider an equally intimate sexual relationship with their sons—it is still incumbent on parents and teachers to discuss sex and sexual skills with the young people in their care as openly and as fully as they can. Sexual inhibitions are passed on from generation to generation. Sexually repressed parents breed sexually maladjusted children, and the resulting unhappiness almost always has repercussions that affect not only the children but *their* children, and those who are intimately associated with them.

6

Teach Yourself
Sexual Skills

Few parents would permit their children to drive without giving them the basic skills to control an automobile and as much of their own experience and practical knowledge as possible. Yet without a qualm they allow them to go out into the world when they're old enough to have sexual relations— or even legally old enough to get married—without making any effort to give them the basic skills of lovemaking, sexual response, and sexual satisfaction.

I questioned more than 200 young men and women from varying backgrounds and walks of life about the sexual skills that their parents had passed on to them. The answer in almost every case was "None." I then asked them what sexual *knowledge* their parents had passed on to them. Forty-two percent of the women said that their mothers had told them about tampons. Twenty-nine percent of the women said that their mothers had told them where babies came from. Thirty-three percent of both men and women had been told by their parents that they should wear a condom while making love—but only 24 percent had been told that they should wear a condom as a contraceptive, and not just as a shield against AIDS.

The consensus of opinion among all 200 was that the sex education they had received from their parents was "well-meaning, but next to zilch"—that the sex education they had received from school was "biological but nothing to do with how to handle real-life sex relationships"—and that neither teachers nor parents had made any serious attempt to tell them how to enjoy sex, what they could expect to get out of it, or how they could be sure of giving maximum satisfaction to their partners.

As 23-year-old Bonnie, a word-processor operator from Butte, Montana, put it: "It's like there's this big secret, which nobody's going to tell you about. My mom told me all about pregnancy. My dad kind of muttered something about AIDS. At school, they gave us lectures about babies being born, with all these slides of smiling families holding each other's hands and showing off everything they've got . . . you know the kind of thing, Mom's got a hairy one but kid sister's only got a slit. But it was like this *big secret*, like everybody was embarrassed to talk about it; or maybe they *did* talk about it but they never included me.

"In the end, I discovered that there is no secret, that everybody has roughly the same kind of body, and that everybody does roughly the same kind of thing. It was great. I felt like shouting it out in the street. The whole damn mystery about sex is that there is no mystery . . . that every guy has a penis and every girl has a vagina, and that it's *fun* for the guy to put his penis into the girl's vagina. I mean, how could the human race have built up such a *taboo* about sex?

"I also discovered—and this was through reading a couple of books, including yours, and from having a sensational love affair with a man I really love— that there's nothing terrible or disgusting about the things that two people choose to do together. If it's exciting, if it turns you on, if you both like it . . . then why feel guilty about doing it?

"Nobody ever, ever told me anything about oral sex . . . only my friends at high school and all they ever said was *urrrgggh*, just imagine sucking a guy's *thing*. But I found out, for instance, that sex without oral sex is hardly sex at all. If the man in my life ever stopped going down on me, for example . . . or if I couldn't give him head . . . well, there wouldn't be any point in it, would there? It's a really close, sensitive way of making love, and it's a time when one person wants to pamper the other person, you know? Like they're really being giving and submissive, if you understand what I mean.

"My lover and I were lying in bed a couple of weeks ago watching TV and I had my head in his lap and I was slowly licking and sucking his cock. I was running my tongue around it, and stroking it up and down, and kissing it, and rubbing it all over my face. I was even giving it butterfly-kisses with my eyelashes! But—you know—there was nothing that was dirty or wrong about that. Most sex books you read, they seem to be telling you that every time you make love, it's got to be this grandstanding fuck, stars and fireworks and whatever. But you don't always feel like it, sometimes you want to do nothing but lick and love and suck and act nice to each other. But *no* teacher ever tells you that. Nor do your parents. I can't imagine my mother saying, 'Well, Bonnie, I really loved to glom your daddy's dick while we were watching *The Man from U.N.C.L.E.* But she could have *mentioned* that you can make love with your mouth. She could have pointed me in the right direction, at least."

If they *do* acquire the skills of loving early, young people almost always find that the benefits remain with them throughout their sexual life. They have longer and more satisfying sexual relationships and a significantly lower divorce rate. They are calmer, more confident, less stressed; and so are their partners.

Interestingly, they are more conventionally moral. In other words, they believe in long-term relationships that are loving and friendly as well as sexual; and when they do get married, a high percentage report that their marriages are "lasting and satisfying."

It is simply not true that the early acquisition of sexual knowledge and sexual skills leads to promiscuity and the breakup of traditional social values. In fact, the opposite is true. Young men and women who are sexually skilled and knowledgeable at an early age are far less likely to seek "cheap thrills" because they know that they can get all the thrills they want with their steady partner. And although the variety and eroticism of their sexual activities may sound startling to those who have never been sexually enlightened, they recognize—as Bonnie recognized—that "sometimes you want to do nothing but lick and love and suck and act nice to each other."

Almost all of the girls that I have ever talked to who have had very early sexual experience have been chronically ignorant about the physical and emotional implications of a sexual relationship. Boys, too. They talk with confidence and bravado, but almost none of them understands that they have done little more than take a first wobbly ride on a kiddie cycle without training wheels, and that (if they fail to broaden their sexual knowledge and their sexual ability) they will never advance beyond that level, and that they will never enjoy sex at its fullest, either physically or emotionally.

That Scary First Experience

Sexual initiation has to go hand-in-hand with open and uninhibited sexual education and sexual training. I won't pretend for a moment that frank sexual discussion doesn't require a great deal of confidence—sometimes even *courage*—on the part of a parent or teacher. How it's done will depend very much on the individuals involved, and their family background and upbringing.

In the closing years of the twentieth century, sex is still a subject fraught with superstition, inhibition, trauma, and insecurity. It is extremely difficult, even today, for young people to get a balanced view not only of what sex is all about, but how to get the best out of it. Yet it only takes one negative sexual experience—particularly if it happens early in our sex lives—to affect our sexual attitudes for the rest of our lives.

I can't count the number of women whose first sexual experience left them withdrawn and fearful. "It was so unsatisfying . . . I didn't even realize that he had put it in me." "It hurt . . . he was so rough . . . it was more like a fight than making love." "The very first time we went to bed together, I was expecting flowers and fireworks. Instead, it was like being attacked. He was so violent. He hurt my breasts, he forced his way up into my vagina before I was ready . . . he squeezed me and bruised my arms . . . and then, right in the middle of the night, when I was sleeping, and I thought it was all over, he started poking his fingers up me. I can't tell you how upset I was, but he kept on saying 'what's the matter with you, are you frigid or something?' When it was all over he asked me if I loved him. *Loved* him? What do you think? I didn't make love to another man for over two years."

"I loved John very much. We'd even talked about getting married. Finally his parents went away for the weekend and we were able to be alone together. I bought new underwear and a new nightdress and everything. We took a bottle of wine to bed, and kissed each other and John undressed me. I felt like I was on my honeymoon. Then we got into bed and he climbed on top of me and put himself inside me. It was everything that I'd imagined it was going to be. It was wonderful. He kissed me and told me he loved me . . . then he went soft. There was nothing that he could do to make it hard again.

"John lost his temper. Frustration, I guess, but of course he blamed me, and I was so innocent I really thought it was my fault . . . you know, something that I'd done wrong. We had a terrible fight and I left. We dated once or twice after that but it didn't work out. For a long time afterwards I didn't date anybody because I really thought I couldn't make love properly, and that no man was going to be able to have a sexual relationship with me. I was real fortunate in having a very understanding sports teacher. I was talking about boys and dating with her one day, and we got around to the subject of sex. I told her I didn't think I'd ever be able to have a proper sexual relationship, and of course she asked me why. When I told her about John she was very understanding. She made me see that it hadn't been my fault . . . and that John had simply been suffering from anxiety.

"Of course if we'd already been told something about sexual problems, we could have worked things out pretty easily. As it was, we blew our whole relationship because of ignorance . . . because we simply didn't *know*."

Even if a parent or teacher finds it difficult to discuss sex face to face, there are many frank and explicit sexual manuals that young people can read—to my knowledge, however, this book is the first that's geared to helping you reach the very peak of your sexual potential.

Of course, sexual instruction will always be a contentious point. I've had discussions with parents and educators who have said to me, "Are you seriously suggesting that I allow my 16-year-old son or daughter to read a book which discusses masturbation, penile and vaginal exercises, how to improve their climaxes, better kissing, oral sex, anal stimulation, sex toys . . . even sexual variations like bondage and role-playing and wet sex?"

My own argument is that the sooner young people have a clear and comprehensive knowledge and understanding of sex and sexual skills, the more satisfying and balanced their love lives are going to be, and the better their chances of reaching the very peak of sexual pleasure. The golden rule is to teach them that however extreme a sexual variation may be, it should always be enjoyed in the context of a rewarding and sharing relationship—not necessarily a long-term relationship—but a relationship in which each partner respects the other's feelings and desires, and, yes, the other's dislikes and inhibitions, too.

Young people are at their physical peak; with good training and good education, they can reach an early sexual peak, too—and continue to improve that performance for the rest of their active sex lives.

Here's Jack, a 19-year-old medical student from Florissant, Missouri: "I guess that being a medical student gives you an edge when it comes to sex, because you have to know all about the human body as a matter of course. Frankly I'm amazed how ignorant my contemporaries are about their own bodies, especially about their sexual responses, but I guess you can't really blame them because their parents are too embarrassed to tell them anything about lovemaking, and their teachers don't see it as part of their job. It's incredible really because the parents of today were the kids of the 1960s, when everything was supposed to be so permissive. Maybe things weren't so permissive after all. Maybe they're still not particularly permissive. They're not very permissive in Florissant, Missouri, I can tell you for an absolute fact. And let's face up to it, these wild and promiscuous brat-pack kids you read about, the ones with the rich Hollywood movie producers for parents, they're only a tiny minority. Most young people today live in a suburban situation with suburban-type morals; and what they aspire to is love and security and happiness. I mean, if you can achieve those three things, what else is there? Well, maybe fame.

"Whatever I do—study, sport, whatever—I always try to give it my best shot. I like to swim, I like to work out, I like football. I'm pretty fit, but not superfit. I like to keep my mind in shape as well as my body.

"I met Fran when we were in high school. She's 17 now, and in a whole lot of ways she's pretty mature for her age. I have to tell you that I fell for her from day one. Not just day one—*minute* one. She has this gorgeous chestnut hair, and just the kind of face I like, green eyes, high cheekbones—and she's real slim; she can wear practically anything and look like a dream.

"We dated for about three months before we did anything more than kiss. When I first went out with her, I was really clumsy at kissing, and she always used to complain that while I was pushing my tongue into her mouth, I never backed off and let her push her tongue into mine. You'd be surprised how many guys do that. They don't realize it's the one chance they've got to have a woman penetrate them, instead of the other way around. Pretty sexy when you think about it, yes?

"Anyway, we went to a party one real hot evening in August last year, and when it was late and most everybody had gone home, we decided to go for a swim. The pool was dark . . . we took off all of our clothes, and swam up and down for a while. Then we stood in the shallow end and kissed. It was the first time that I'd held Fran in my arms completely naked. Of course my cock was sticking out about a mile. She took hold of it in her hand and rubbed it against her pubic hair, and rolled it against her bare stomach. She held it so naturally that she turned me on even more. I think I had bells and sirens ringing in my head!

"She Used a Dirty Word"

"I kissed her. Her hair was all wet and she tasted of swimming pool. I can remember cupping her breasts in my hands. She has these very small breasts, little tiny ones, but her nipples were all crinkled and sticking up, and I circled them around and around in the palms of my hands, and tugged them between my fingers.

"We kissed some more and then she whispered in my ear, 'Fuck me, Jack, please.' I think it was the fact that she used a dirty word that excited me more than anything. I knew for a fact that she was a virgin, but of course all the girls in her class talked dirty, so she knew what all the words meant.

"We climbed out of the pool and spread out some towels on the grass, behind the barbecue, where nobody could see us. They must have thought that we'd gone home already, because they started switching off all the lights in the house, and I could hear them locking up.

"We were left in the garden on our own. It was mostly dark, but we lay down next to a light in one of the flowerbeds. Nobody could see us from the house. Fran lay on the towel with her hands crossed over her breasts. I had to get my one and only Trojan out of my billfold. I stood beside her and rolled it over the glans of my cock . . . but she sat up and said, 'Here . . . I want to do it.' So she rolled the condom over my shaft, and held my balls in her hand like they were some kind of strange fruit that she'd heard about but never touched.

"I laid her down on the towels and kissed her and stroked her hair and kissed her nipples and everything. Then I opened up her thighs and pushed my cock up against her cunt. I pushed once or twice but she felt real tight and dry . . . almost as if she wasn't aroused at all. I thought, 'Oh, shit . . . this is all falling apart.'

"But then I thought of some of the things I'd read, and some of the things I'd been taught. There was something in one of your books—I think it was *How to Drive Your Woman Wild in Bed*—and it had always stuck in my mind because I thought it sounded very masterful at the time. Some guy was describing how he always pleased his girlfriends by taking things real slow . . . so slow that after a while they would be practically *sobbing* for him to put it in. I remembered something else, too . . . that girls who are uptight about making love quite often prefer to sit on top. It makes them feel more in control of what's going on . . . less *pressed-on*, even though you can hold their hips in your hand and pump them up and down on your cock just as forcefully as if you're lying on top of them. Another thing, too, I remembered, was that in the girl-on-top position the guy can fondle her breasts more easily and caress her body more easily because he's got both hands free . . . he's not using his arms to support his own weight.

"And I *also* remembered that a girl can get much more turned-on when she's sitting on top because she can control exactly how far your cock goes up inside her. She can lean forward if she doesn't want it up too far, or sit up straight if she wants it right up to her womb.

"Now, all of that was knowledge that I'd acquired from reading one of your books. Not the kind of information you usually get from your good old dad, is it, or your friendly high school biology teacher? I rolled over on my side, onto the towels, and I lifted Fran on top of me. I didn't worry about putting myself inside her, not to begin with. I kissed her and let her kiss me in return, and I caressed her back—now *that's* something else I learned from that book, caressing a woman's back can really get her nerves tingling.

"She took hold of my cock and rubbed it up and down, and I have to tell you that when you're wearing a condom, a little bit of extra hand stimulation doesn't do you any harm at all. After a while, I reached down between Fran's legs and I could feel that her pussy was all wet and slippery. I stroked her labia and I gently played with her clitoris, and she began to get wetter still. She climbed right on top of me then and she was breathing real quick. I had both hands down between her legs and I was caressing her labia and sliding my fingers up inside her vagina.

"I have to tell you, inside her vagina, she felt like heaven. Soft, hot, tight, and slippery with juice. I kissed her, and kept on sliding my fingers in and out, but she kissed me back so hard that I could feel her teeth behind her lips, and she took hold of my cock and said, 'Fuck me, fuck me, you've got to fuck me.'

"I opened up her labia with my two fingers and immediately she pushed my rubber-covered glans right up against her vagina. Now she was ready . . . now she was more than ready, and I was, too. She held the shaft of my cock real tight, so that I felt as if my glans was practically going to burst. I could see the purple skin through the rubber, turning even more purple. Then Fran eased herself down, and my glans sank into the shiny pink lips of her pussy, followed by the shaft. She sat down on me, really sat down on me, so that I could feel her wet labia lapping from side to side on my bare balls. My cock was totally buried in the warmth of her body: I could feel the neck of her womb rubbing against my glans. I said something like, 'Fran, I think I've died and gone to heaven,' but all she did was lean forward and lick my face and kiss me.

"She tried to ride me faster and faster. But all the time I held her hips and made her go slow. That way, the feeling really had time to build up. We had time to relish it. This was her first-ever fuck, and I wanted her to think back on it one day and say it was the first and the best. She lifted herself up so that my cock was only just inside her, her labia just clinging on to the wet rubber-covered head. She tried to force herself back down again, but I held her up for a moment longer, until she was gasping out, 'Please, Jack, please,' and then I let her slide herself down and my cock disappeared up inside her again.

"She sat up straight, so that my cock went up as deep as possible, and swayed and rolled her hips around. I looked up at her, my hands squeezing and caressing her breasts. Her head was thrown right back and her lips were shining. Then suddenly she started to whimper, and quake. She bunched up her fists and hunched her shoulders and her whole body went into a spasm. Her nipples stuck out unbelievably hard.

"The inside of her vagina clenched and unclenched, and even though I'd wanted to hold on longer, and maybe give her two orgasms instead of just one, she sent me right over the edge. I felt that sperm jetting up the whole length of my cock, and filling that condom deep inside her. Three full jets, great big squirts of sperm, and then two or three small ones.

"I took my cock out immediately. I didn't want to take any risks. Fran clung to me and kissed me and even though she was sweating she was shivering, too. She said, 'I never even guessed. I never even guessed. We should have done it *months* ago!'

"I was going to slip off my condom, but when she saw what I was doing she said, 'No . . . let me. I never saw it before.' She gently pulled the condom off my cock, which was just about half-soft by now . . . or maybe still half-hard, depends on whether you're a pessimist or an optimist, I guess.

"She turned the condom inside out, so that the sperm filled the palm of her hand. She rubbed it around and around with her fingertips, and then she smelled it. 'It smells beautiful,' she said. 'Kind of rubbery with a condom,' I told her, but she didn't seem to mind. It was amazing, watching somebody discover something for the first time. She'd never seen a man's sperm before, let alone held a handful of it. She kissed me again, and then she smeared the sperm all over her breasts, massaging her nipples with it. 'Julie told me it makes your breasts grow bigger,' she said.

" 'Old wives' tale,' I told her.

"To me, yes, that was sex to the max, especially considering the facts that we'd never made love before, that it was Fran's very first time, and that it was outdoors, and that I had to wear a condom. I guess that any one of those factors could have been enough to turn the whole thing into a disaster . . . or if not a disaster, the kind of fiasco that would have made Fran think that sex was pretty disgusting, or that it wasn't such a big deal, after all.

"Fran says that plenty of her girlfriends have frequent sex, but don't honestly think that it's anything special. I've talked to some of their boyfriends, and believe me I can see why. You wonder what they're going to be like in five, ten, twenty years' time. Still fumbling away like they are now. Or maybe so bored with it they don't even do it anymore."

Although Jack, for a 19-year-old, sometimes sounded overopinionated and a little too pleased with himself, he had at least understood that lovemaking isn't just a question of doing what comes naturally. Humans are the only species who have sex for recreational and emotional purposes—and because of that the stimulation we seek and need can often be highly complex. One night, for example, a man may feel the urge to make love to his partner quite aggressively—not because he feels violent or aggressive toward her, but because he is aroused by the vigorous and macho feeling of ramming his hardened penis into her soft and defenseless body. The next time they make love, the same man may feel like lying back and having his lover make all the advances. Of course, problems arise when his lover doesn't feel like being aggressively fucked on the night that he feels like aggressively fucking her; or like making all the moves on the night when he feels like lying back and having it all done to him.

Working out who feels like what—and when—and what you both should do about it, is the key to peak-performance sex. As I have said before, you yourself may be physically fit, skillful and knowledgeable, and emotionally well-attuned, but it's how you and your lover bring your skills together that makes all the difference between lovemaking that's okay and lovemaking that's spectacular.

Here's Debbie, a 17-year-old high school student from Santa Cruz, California: "I'm very fit because I jog and work out and I'm very active in school athletics. I'm proud of my body and I'm proud of myself. As far as sexual skill is concerned obviously I'm very young and you learn as you go along. But my parents were always very open with me when it came to talking about sex, and when I was about fourteen my mom told me all about lovemaking and what I could expect out of a sexual relationship.

"In no way did that make me rush out and have a sexual relationship immediately, because she also told me all about masturbation—and that when you felt a strong sexual urge you can always satisfy yourself that way. A lot of the girls at school believed all kinds of weird stories about masturbation—like you'd never be able to have proper sex with a man if you masturbated—or your hair would start falling out, or your periods would dry up; but Mom told me that masturbation was totally harmless, in fact it could even be good for you because it helped you to discover your own body, and what an orgasm felt like, and not to be afraid to touch yourself sexually. I didn't masturbate every minute of the day just because I knew about it—any more than I went off and went straight to bed with boys just because I knew about it. I don't think *knowing* about sex makes you depraved or anything. In fact I think the opposite is true. All of my friends whose parents never told them much about sex always seem to be the ones who wind up in the most trouble with boys.

"I first had sex with a boy the day after my sixteenth birthday. His name was Ted, and I'd known him ever since we were kids. Both his parents were working, so we went around to his house and played records and made ourselves pizza and drank wine. We felt very grown-up, I remember.

"We kissed and petted a whole lot, and then we undressed and lay on the floor in front of the open patio doors. I was amazed by the size of Ted's cock . . . I'd never seen a boy with a hard-on before. I kissed him and stroked him and everything, trying to take it slow and easy. That was one thing my mom had told me about lovemaking . . . don't rush it, take it slow and easy, relish every moment. I tried to, but Ted was so frantic and anxious. He climbed on top of me, and tried to push his cock in before he'd even kissed me. I said, 'Ssh, Ted, take it easy, relax.' I took hold of his cock in my hand and the next thing I knew he was spurting semen all over me.

"We tried again later, but he'd lost his confidence. Sometimes I think that I should have let him do it the way he wanted to, real quick, and then work on our sexual relationship from there. But I was just as inexperienced as he was . . . the only difference was that I *had* had some good advice.

"I'm going steady with Paul now, he's 19. The first time Paul and I made love, I didn't think I'd ever get used to it, he seemed to have such a different rhythm than mine. But after two or three times, we began to work together, and now we have really terrific sex. Well, you talked about peak-performance sex . . . I think that's what we've got.

"The time that really stands out in my mind was when we went down to the beach together early one morning. We'd only planned to swim, but when we got there, the whole beach was deserted. It was a beautiful warm day, and since there was nobody around we went skinny-dipping. Paul chased me all around the sand and into the sea, and we swam for a while . . . then we came back onto the beach and dried ourselves and spread out our blanket and put up our beach umbrella.

"I stood up to change the angle of the beach umbrella, when Paul sat up behind me, and kissed my bottom. I said 'Mmm, that's nice,' and I poked my bottom out a bit more. He kissed my bottom-cheeks and he stroked my thighs, and then he opened up my cheeks a little way and ran his tongue all the way down the cleft of my bottom and started tonguing my anus. He licked all around it, and then he pushed the tip of his tongue right inside. Nobody had ever done that to me before . . . it felt really weird but *very* erotic.

"Then he ducked his head down right between my legs and started licking my cunt. He'd done that before, but not out in the open air. I held onto that beach umbrella for balance, and spread my thighs wider and wider, and there he was kneeling between my legs licking at my cunt like a puppy. I mean the feeling was fantastic, just fantastic. I could feel the breeze and the wet and the tickle of his hair, and I looked down and I could see my own cunt juice running down his chin.

"Then he stood up, and took hold of me from behind, around my waist, and slid his cock right up inside me, smooth and hard. I kept holding on to the beach umbrella, and he fucked me then and there, standing up. We both got this fantastic rhythm going, almost like a dance rhythm, like the *lambada*—his cock sliding in and out of my cunt, sliding in so far that I practically cried because it felt so good.

"We were like one person, really flowing together. I bent forward and touched my toes while he fucked me, and I could see his balls bobbing against me, all tight and scrunched-up and ready to shoot.

"That was the first orgasm I ever had standing up. Paul had to hold on to me to stop from falling over. I think I screamed. Paul held me tight in his arms and I literally jumped up and down on his cock like a puppet on a string. It was just amazing . . . and what made it so amazing was that we were both so *close*."

Sex Like Dancing

Debbie's description of making love "almost like a dance rhythm" shows how far she had managed to develop her sexual skill, despite being so young. Dancing is intimate, amusing, pleasurable, rhythmic . . . and if more lovers could think about sex as dancing rather than fighting, they would achieve peak-performance sex much more quickly and much more easily.

We've discussed how sexual skills should be developed early, but age is no bar to achieving highly erotic and satisfying sex. Provided you keep reasonably fit, there is no reason why you shouldn't be able to enjoy intensely arousing sexual experiences throughout your life. Some of the most skillful lovers I have met have been well into their seventies. What they may lack in physical resilience and stamina they more than make up for with sexual ingenuity and experience.

We'll take a look at sex for the older lover later on. Meanwhile, let's examine some common sexual problems that make it difficult for lovers of all ages to achieve peak performance in bed, and which have to be solved before they can start improving their love lives.

7

How to Solve Your Sex Problems . . . Yourself

"I thought we had a terrific sex life. I thought Susan always enjoyed our lovemaking. She always *seemed* to enjoy it. Then one day we had an argument over something real stupid, like whether I'd paid a credit card bill or not, and she practically went crazy. She told me that I was the most boring man she had ever known—and what was worse, I was boring in bed."

This is Mike, a 29-year-old electronics engineer from St. Paul, Minnesota, talking about his sexual problems with his wife Susan, 25. He admitted that he had "kind of a staid personality" and that he could accept criticism that he wasn't always the most exciting company. But he couldn't understand what he was doing wrong in bed.

"All right, I wasn't Casanova. But I kissed her and gave her plenty of caresses and foreplay, just like they tell you in the books. I always made sure she was well aroused before I entered her, and I always tried to make sure that she was satisfied."

It did't take long for me to realize what Mike's problem was. He was *always* considerate. He was *always* careful to make sure that Susan's vagina was well lubricated before he inserted his penis. He *always* asked her, "How did you like that, darling?" What was worse, he always made love in the same position—him on top, her underneath.

He was a thoughtful lover, yes—but he had allowed his thoughtfulness to become a routine, and if there is one thing that dampens a sexual affair quicker than a pail full of cold water, it's routine. Sex is an expression of how you feel about your partner: it should always be surprising, different, spontaneous, passionate. Sometimes a man will want a woman so much that he won't bother to test her vaginal lubrication before he pushes himself into her (although it's surprising how often a woman *will* already be wet if a man has shown her how much he wants her.) Sometimes a woman won't want to wait for her mate to take a shower and clip his nose hairs in the bathroom mirror and roll on his Mennen Speedstick. Sometimes she'll want him to lift up her skirt and pull the gusset of her panties to one side and just fuck her.

Of course, all long-term sexual relationships are prone to becoming routine. Lovers become lazy, and start to take each other for granted. But if you take the trouble to vary your lovemaking occasionally, you will find that the rewards vastly outweigh the effort.

One common problem is that a man often believes that his lover would be shocked or disgusted by different sexual acts. "I know that Marjorie doesn't mind different positions now and again," said 34-year-old Hector, an automobile salesman from El Paso, Texas, "but I couldn't ask her to do any of that oral sex. If I tried to go down on her—well, I think she'd be shocked. I don't even know what she'd do, but I think she'd be shocked, certainly. I certainly can't imagine Marjorie taking my penis in her mouth. Can't imagine it, no way. And certainly not anal."

Would he enjoy his sex life more if she did give him oral sex and other variations? "Well, of course. But she's not the kind of woman."

On a separate occasion, I talked to Marjorie. Did she consider her love life satisfying? exciting? ordinary? routine? dull?

"Lovemaking isn't what the books and the magazines and the movies all crack it up to be."

In what way?

"They make it out to be exciting, but it isn't particularly. In fact I sometimes wonder why Hector bothers at all. He doesn't have much of a sex drive. He's very cautious and withdrawn when it comes to making love. I think sex embarrasses him."

Have you ever thought about introducing a little variety into your sex life? Say, oral sex? Or maybe a little dressing up, or role playing, or simply making love in a different and exciting location?

"I don't honestly think that Hector would go for that."

How about you? Do you have any inhibitions about sex?

"Tied Naked to a Tree"

"None that I know of, except that I don't like the idea of sadism—you know, people hurting each other for pleasure. I have a fantasy about being tied naked to a tree in the woods, you know, and whatever man comes along can use me however he likes, and there's nothing that I can do to stop him. Sometimes I even think about being tied up naked to a tree and two men come along at once, and they both take me. Sometimes even three, or four, or five. One of my friends told me that when she was younger she'd made love to two boys at once, and a friend of hers had made love to *five*—two up her backside, one in her vagina, and two in her mouth, all at once."

Is there anything she wouldn't do with Hector?

"For myself, no. But I think Hector finds sex difficult. I wouldn't even dare to give him oral sex. He'd think I was some kind of whore."

The lack of sexual communication between Hector and Marjorie was almost total—but not at all unusual. Literally millions of sexual relationships never develop beyond straightforward and highly inhibited lovemaking because each partner is shy of the other. One of the first steps in achieving peak-performance sex is for both partners to sit down and openly discuss what physical urges you have and whether you feel they're being satisfied. This has to be a no-holds-barred discussion, in which you reveal all of your unfulfilled desires, all of your fantasies and fetishes, all of those dark and erotic thoughts that stimulate you most. Obviously, one discussion won't be enough. It will take time for you to consider and discuss the sexual needs that (previously) you kept to yourselves. There may be shock. There may be disgust. There may be arguments. But it's a very constructive and worthwhile process, and nothing but positive results can eventually come out of it—both for your physical satisfaction and your emotional contentment.

When I persuaded Hector and Marjorie to sit down and talk to each other about sex, they were astonished that they *both* should have imagined for so long that their lover was so sexually inhibited.

But the latest report I had before writing this chapter was that their sex life had been "practically transformed . . . it's like magic." Marjorie said that they regularly enjoyed oral sex, and that she had been initiated into anal sex while tied to a gate at a friend's ranch. (Incidentally, if there are any disbelievers about the five-men-at-once story, former porno star Linda Lovelace once remarked about two notably well-hung studs with whom she played, "I've taken both their cocks into my mouth at one time, and have also taken them both in my ass— together, I mean." Of course Linda Lovelace had a more-than-average appetite for sex in those days, but many of the sexual skills and sexual exercises she developed are just as relevant and useful for the average couple who want to get the best out of their sex lives.)

Many lovers are reluctant to face up to the fact that they need to discuss their sexual problems at all. But you can assess the openness and intimacy of *your* sexual relationship if both of you answer the following questions *with complete honesty.* You are allowed to pass on three questions *without being questioned by your lover as to why you decided to pass*), but you may decide that your "pass" questions could well be the subject of future discussion.

WHAT ARE YOU HIDING FROM YOUR SEX PARTNER?

1. Sometimes our lovemaking leaves me feeling frustrated. YES/NO/PASS
2. Sometimes I would like to try lovemaking in another locality. YES/NO/PASS
3. I have sexual fantasies during lovemaking which I would be hesitant to describe to my lover. YES/NO/PASS

4. There are certain things that irritate me about the way in which my lover makes love. YES/NO/PASS

5. I would like my lover to undress me more often. YES/NO/PASS

6. I would like my lover to say romantic things to me more often. YES/NO/PASS

7. My lover never kisses me enough. YES/NO/PASS

8. My lover's foreplay is often too hurried. YES/NO/PASS

9. My lover never bothers with foreplay. YES/NO/PASS

10. I wish my lover would sometimes caress me without making me feel that we have to have intercourse. YES/NO/PASS

11. I wish my lover would give me oral sex more often. YES/NO/PASS

12. I wish my lover would give me oral sex *at all*. YES/NO/PASS

13. (*for men*) My lover seems to take a very long time to get aroused. YES/NO/PASS

14. (*for women*) My lover often seems to penetrate me before I'm really ready. YES/NO/PASS

15. I dislike some of the things my lover does during lovemaking. YES/NO/PASS

16. I wish my lover were more responsive during sex. YES/NO/PASS

17. I wish my lover would expose him- or herself to me more openly. YES/NO/PASS

18. I would like to watch sex videos during lovemaking, but I'm not sure that my lover would. YES/NO/PASS

19. Sometimes I'm tempted to buy sex toys, but I'm not sure my lover would like them. YES/NO/PASS

20. I have a secret sexual yearning that I am not sure that my lover would enjoy. YES/NO/PASS

21. My secret sexual yearning is connected with one or more of the following (check those that apply) (i) sex in unusual places☐ (ii) erotic lingerie such as basques, stockings, and garter belts☐ (iii) leatherwear☐ (iv) rubberwear☐ (v) spanking☐ (vi) bondage☐ (vii) uniforms (nurse's, military, etc.)☐ (viii) oral sex☐ (ix) playing out sex fantasies such as slave and slavemaster, mistress and servant, sheik and harem girl, etc.☐ (x) masturbation, single or mutual☐ (xi) watching or reading pornography together☐ (xii) making sex videos or taking erotic photographs of each other☐ (xiii) pubic shaving☐ (xiv) wet sex☐ (xv) anal sex☐ (xvi) other (specify)——

22. There are points about my lover's physical appearance that could be improved. YES/NO/PASS

23. I wish my lover would make an effort to be more fit. YES/NO/PASS

24. An improvement to my lover's personal hygiene could make him or her more sexually attractive to me. YES/NO/PASS

25. I wish my lover would take the trouble to find out what turns me on. YES/NO/PASS

26. There are certain sexual things that I know my lover wants me to do, but I don't want to do them and so I feign ignorance or unresponsiveness. YES/NO/PASS

27. I wish my lover were more flirtatious and made more effort to seduce me. YES/NO/PASS

28. I would like to examine and caress my lover's genitalia closely and unhurriedly. YES/NO/PASS

29. Sometimes I wish my lover would make the first move in bed. YES/NO/PASS

30. I think that my lover and I could improve our sex life if we were more open with each other. YES/NO/PASS

There are no "right" or "wrong" answers to this questionnaire—it's designed simply for you both to fill out, to compare, and then to use as a basis for further discussion. For instance, if a woman checked #21 (viii), there is obviously much more to be talked out between you than simply "oral sex." Does she want her lover to give her oral sex, or would she like to give him oral sex? There are some men who dislike the idea of kissing and licking their lover's vulvas, either because they don't enjoy the taste or because they feel that it's somehow demeaning for them to put their face down between their lover's thighs. I had a lengthy correspondence with one 25-year-old wife from Boston, whose husband had once enjoyed giving her oral sex (cunnilingus) but had then suddenly stopped. She couldn't understand why and he was touchy enough for her not to want to press him on the subject. It turned out in the end that he had been sucking her clitoris and looking up at her, and that she had been amused by how much her pubic hair looked like a mustache. She had laughed, and he had never given her oral sex again, even though he enjoyed it.

I suggested that the wife shave her pubic hair, which she did. She wrote later to say that everything had worked out better than expected. She liked being shaved, her husband thought it was a tremendous turn-on, and normal cunnilingus had been enthusiastically restored, to the pleasure and satisfaction of both partners.

To Swallow or Not to Swallow?

A trickier problem with oral sex arose when a 21-
year-old woman from Berkeley, California, asked my
advice on the subject of swallowing semen. She
enjoyed giving her 26-year-old boyfriend a frequent
"blowjob" (fellatio) and she knew that it gave him
intense pleasure. The only trouble was, she didn't
like the taste or the consistency of semen. Some
women love it, some women don't care about it one
way or the other, some women hate it.

She had tried to make it clear to her boyfriend
that she didn't enjoy swallowing it, but as he neared
his climax he always held her head—not so much
forcefully as firmly—so that without making a considerable effort to break free from him, she had no
choice. Quite rightly, she found this coercion to be
bullying and disagreeable. So—she had stopped fellating him, turning away when he suggestively
reared his penis close to her face—and although he
hadn't yet openly complained, she could sense his
increasing disappointment and frustration.

As I've said so often, all sexual acts should be
enjoyed not just by one partner but by *both*. One
partner may enjoy a particular sexual act more than
the other, and the other partner should enjoy giving
so much pleasure, and be able to look forward to
receiving just as much pleasure in return.

So our Berkeley woman had every right to refuse
to swallow her boyfriend's semen, and every right to
tell him why. Incidentally, semen is quite harmless if
swallowed . . . it's composed mainly of simple
sugars.

After I had written to her, she managed to discuss
it with her boyfriend, and although he was indig-
nant at first, his mood soon changed when she dem-

onstrated my suggested alternative (to which she had enthusiastically agreed). This alternative was simply that—when he ejaculated—he should take his penis out of her mouth and ejaculate on her face or breasts.

"The whole mood's changed," she wrote back. "I always loved licking and sucking his cock, and now I can do it without that feeling in the back of my mind that he's going to shoot it all down my throat. When he sprays it out, it's wonderful. I hold his cock so that he shoots it straight into my face, onto my cheeks and forehead and my lips, and it slides down my face all warm and sticky and let me tell you *it turns me on.*"

8

The Look of Love

A common obstacle to achieving peak-performance sex is simply a lack of sexual knowledge. You may think that, these days, there is no excuse for either men or women to be ignorant about sex. After all, plenty of advice books are available, as well as magazine articles and TV discussions. Twenty years ago, when I wrote the first edition of *How to Drive Your Man Wild in Bed*, a young man or woman who wanted to know what the genitalia of the opposite sex looked like had difficulty in obtaining any suitable pictorial material. I'm not talking about the drawings and diagrams of sex organs that appear in sex encyclopedias and medical books. Although they're useful for instructional purposes and the "naming of parts," they give you no idea of the true appearance of a penis or a vulva, or how varied our genitalia can be.

Today, of course, scores of magazines are available that show women with their legs wide apart—and a lesser number of magazines that contain photographs of nude men. The taboo of these publications, in my opinion, is created only in the minds of those who have unwarranted inhibitions about sex. I certainly don't think that they should be foisted on people who don't want to see them, but I do believe that they ought to be freely available to those who do. An afternoon in the company of a mature and comprehensive sex manual and a few copies of *Hustler* and *Playgirl* can work wonders for a man or woman *of any age* who has questions about sex and the human body.

In later chapters, we'll take a peak-performance look at the male and female bodies—how they function sexually, and how to improve that function. But as I mentioned earlier, one of the most interesting new ways in which both singles and couples can enlarge their basic knowledge of their own bodies and their own sexual performance is by using a video camcorder.

For singles, a large mirror is invaluable. Rest it against a chair or the side of your bed so that you can sit comfortably in front of it with your legs apart and clearly see your genitals. Angle the mirror so that your genitals are brightly illuminated by sunlight or a desk lamp. A tripod to support your camcorder is well worth the small investment, but you can just as easily set it up on a chair or table so that it is focused where you want it—or you can hold it in one hand during your exercises, although this is obviously less satisfactory.

It will help you to understand what you are seeing and doing if you have already read up on the subject of sexual anatomy. I particularly recommend the chapters on sexual self-exploration in my last book, *How to Make Love Six Nights a Week*. Many girls in particular are unsure of their sexual anatomy, partly because their genitalia are very much more concealed than boys', and they have had far less opportunity to inspect the genitalia of other girls and make comparisons, even though girls' vulvas vary just as widely in appearance and shape and even *color* as boys' penises.

You will see from the most cursory inspection of a man's magazine that some women have very prominent mounds of Venus, whereas others—especially those of younger girls who haven't yet had children—are very flat. Some women have large and fleshy vaginal lips. I have several photographs that show a young woman whose inner lips are so long that she can stretch them out at least three inches on each side of her vagina, and another set of photographs showing a young woman whose lips are narrow and small.

Some women have darkly pigmented vulvas; others are reddish; others are pale pink. There is no such thing as a standard vulva, any more than there is a standard face or a standard pair of breasts.

Men's sexual organs differ enormously in shape and size, and—again—in pigmentation. Dark-haired men usually have darkly pigmented penises. Sometimes they can look almost as if they've been tanning them through a hole in a fence, as one lady of my acquaintance put it. The shape of the penis head, or glans, can differ from sharply wedge-shaped to dome-shaped; and a man's foreskin (if he hasn't been circumcized) can vary from a long tassel-like piece that extends beyond the glans to a stretched piece of skin that barely covers it—or only half-covers it.

Some glans are pale purple, some are crimson, some are brown. The color has no effect on how they function—just as a vibrator works just as well whether it's molded out of pink plastic or blue.

Even the shafts of penises are very different. When they're erect, some bend slightly to the right or the left (this is well within the parameters of human variation, very common and quite harmless—so don't go trying to straighten them out, chaps).

Some shafts are thin and narrow, whereas others are fat and curved. Even scrotal sacs vary—in color, in size, in looseness, in tightness. Balls, or testes, come in all sizes and shapes, too, but provided they function you have nothing to worry about. Not everybody can have the equipment of a Rhesus monkey.

Over the years, I have received more queries and questions about the appearance of sexual organs than almost any other subject. Women have asked me if their clitorises are in the correct position. Some women have even said that they don't believe they *have* a clitoris. Men are eternally anxious about their size. "I don't think that I'll be able to satisfy my girlfriend," wrote a pessimistic swain who had measured himself and found that he was only 5½ inches long, when fully erect. Women worry about their men's sizes, too. "He seems to have such a small one, I can hardly feel him. Is there anything he can do to enlarge it?"

Of course, all women have clitorises, although the extraordinary variety of differently formed vulvas means that some clitorides stand out prominently, whereas others are almost completely buried in flesh.

Does Penis Size Matter?

And as far as penis size is concerned, all men of whatever size are potentially capable of sexually satisfying all women. Women can be stimulated to orgasm by the insertion of anything from a single ball point pen to a man's entire fist into their vaginas. It isn't penis size that counts, it's sexual skill—and, to a much lesser extent, sexual exercise—on the part of the woman, as well as the man.

These are questions we can discuss later. For now, let's see how two ordinary people used camcorders to explore themselves sexually—what they learned, and how they applied what they learned to improve their sex lives.

This is Maureen, an 18-year-old liberal arts student from Madison, Wisconsin. As the only child of older parents, Maureen had what she called a "closeted" upbringing, and as a young teenager knew very little about sex except for the facts of human reproduction. She said that her parents always gave her the feeling that sex was "kind of unnecessary, and vaguely dirty . . . like they'd prefer the planet Earth a whole lot more if it didn't have sex on it." She said that up until the age of 16, her mental image of sex had been "sniggering, and toilet seats, and tampons; and my classmates endlessly discussing the size of the bulge in men's jeans."

Maureen had lost her virginity when she was 17½—although she hadn't slept with her boyfriend Mike more than "five or six times." This was not because she didn't enjoy lovemaking, but simply because they were unable to meet very often. She said that she liked sex, but felt strongly that "I'm not at all sure what's happening to me, or what I'm doing. It's like a huge mystery. I have all these powerful physical and emotional feelings but I don't know how to control them or even what I'm supposed to do with them."

In particular, Maureen felt that she didn't know enough about her own body or her boyfriend's body, and what was happening to her when they made love. "It was like discovering that I could suddenly fly, but not knowing how I was able to do it, and not knowing if I could ever do it again."

When her parents went away for the weekend, she set up the camcorder in her bedroom, and loaded it with a new videocassette that she had bought herself. ("I didn't want all the relations to sit down, thinking they were going to watch a video of

Christmas dinner—and then seeing my cunt in living color.")

"I took the mirror from the hallway and propped it up against the bed. I set up my bedside lamp on the floor beside it, and tilted the shade so that it would shine directly between my legs. We don't have a stand for the video camera so I put it on my dressing-table stool and angled it with two books underneath it. Then I undressed. For some reason I felt short of breath and very guilty, and even though it was warm in the house I shivered. When I sat on the floor in front of the mirror I had goosebumps and my nipples were hard. But I took a few deep breaths, and stared at myself in the mirror and told myself to relax. This was supposed to be learning, and this was supposed to be *fun*.

Following the recommendations that I had given her, Maureen "took stock of herself."

"I looked at my hair and decided that I liked it the way it was. It's a kind of mousy blonde and maybe it needed a little highlighting, but on the whole I liked it. I looked at my face closely, too, and checked all of my *good* points. Big blue eyes, good teeth. I've never liked my nose too much. Too snubby. But the good points outweighed the iffy points.

"My breasts . . . well, I quite like my breasts. I didn't even *have* any breasts until I was fourteen, and by that time most of my schoolfriends were prancing around with 36 double Ds. My breasts are still smallish, but they're firm and they stick up high, and at least I can wear all of the clothes that I want to, while a lot of my girlfriends complain that they can't get into swimsuits or summer dresses and that their breasts always bounce when they jog or play sports.

"As for the rest of me, I'm pretty happy with the

way I am. I'm slim, I think I look pretty good. I never sat down naked in front of a mirror before and really looked myself over. Well, you don't, do you, not normally? But if you do it in a positive frame of mind it can give you confidence. Even if you see things you don't like too much, you can say to yourself . . . okay, that's it, I can see what's wrong, I'm going to make sure that I do something about it. Like, I did go and have my hair highlighted two days later . . . and if I'd put on weight, or my eyebrows need plucking, whatever, I would have done it . . . and then I would have given myself the same all-over check seven days later, just the way you suggested. It's really good to watch yourself making actual progress, something you can write down in your diary, something you can *see*.

"I was *very* unsure about looking at myself sexually, especially in front of the video camera. To begin with I just put my hand down between my legs and kind of cupped myself without actually looking. But then I thought—it's your body, you can do what you like. So I opened my legs wider and looked at myself in the mirror. I had my sex book beside me so that I could tell what everything was. Of course I could see the labia majora, the outer lips. I have very fine blonde pubic hair and I usually trim it very short with nail scissors but I don't need to shave because I'm not very hairy and the sides of my mound are quite bare anyway.

"I opened up my inner lips with the fingers of both hands . . . those are the labia minora, right? Mine are very light pink and quite thin. My whole vulva was very juicy and wet, much juicier than usual—I think because I was aroused by the idea of filming myself. I ran the tips of my fingers lightly down the sides of my lips, in between the labia majora and the labia minora, and then down the middle where my labia minora were still stuck together. I could feel how sensitive the nerves were. My lips felt more sensitive as my fingertip came close to my vagina, and they were definitely more sensitive on the edges than they were at the sides. My juice was slippery but about the consistency of thin honey. When I took my fingertip away from my labia, a thin thread of fluid connected my vagina and my fingertip for a moment, then broke. I smelled and tasted the juice but it didn't taste like anything much. It was a very *clean* taste, though; very slightly sweetish; strange.

"I Stretched Myself Wide Apart"

"I peeled my labia minora apart and exposed my vagina. Inside it was much brighter pink, almost scarlet. I shifted myself around a little so that the camera would get a clear view right up inside my cunt. If you look at the video now you can see the ridges of my vagina walls, and it's all shining and wet. Then I inserted two fingers into my vagina and felt up inside myself as far as I could. The best feeling I got was when I kind of hooked my fingers forward, and pressed rhythmically on the front of my vagina." (In fact at that moment she was stimulating her so-called G-spot, of which more later.) "I liked that feeling so much that I did what you said and closed my eyes and just enjoyed it for a while. I began to get very wet. The juice was pouring out of my cunt and making a damp patch on the rug.

"I took my fingers out and stretched my labia minora wide apart so that I could see my urethra. I knew where it was. I mean, I knew that I peed out of a different hole, even though some of my friends didn't when they were younger. But I had never looked at it so closely. It's not a thing you normally think about doing, is it? I touched myself gently all around it, and there are some very sensitive nerve endings there. I managed to squeeze out a single drop of pee, just to watch it coming out. You suddenly realize not only how incredible your body is, but also how much you can control it.

"My clitoris is quite prominent, the labia minora don't cover it very much, and so that wasn't difficult to find. I tried various different ways of touching it and stroking it. I think the way that gave me the most pleasure was to tease it very gently underneath with the tip of my middle finger, while quickly flicking the shaft of it with the side of my index finger. I did this very, very fast, but very lightly, too, barely touching it. I'd done it before, when I was lying in bed thinking about Bernie [her boyfriend], but I'd never *watched* myself doing it before.

"Next I did the vaginal exercises, just flexing the muscle between my legs to see what effect it had on the shape of my cunt. It's remarkable, isn't it—apart from the fact that if you flex it twenty or thirty times, you begin to feel really turned on! That was what I really discovered by making this video: how much I was capable of controlling my own body sexually. It had never occurred to me, for instance, that if I relaxed my vaginal muscles during lovemaking, Bernie's cock wouldn't be massaged so hard, and so he wouldn't come to a climax so soon. It sounds obvious, I know—but it's one of those things you have to do consciously, one of those things you have to *train* yourself to do. Judging the right moment to do it, I'd say, yes, that's a sexual skill.

"I didn't have a dildo or a vibrator, but I used a large carrot instead. I hope that was okay! I hunkered down, and guided it up into my cunt, as far as it would go. It was actually bigger than Bernie's cock, but you said that didn't matter. I slid it in and out of myself, and tried all kinds of different positions with it—lying on my back with my legs apart, lying on my side, kneeling on all fours doggie-fashion. The position in which it gave me the most stimulation was when I was lying on my side with my legs drawn up. I could reach down and rub my clitoris at the same time . . . or Bernie could do it at the same time that he was making love to me from behind.

"In the end, all this rubbing myself was turning me on so much that I couldn't stop. At the end of the video I'm lying on my back with my legs wide apart, and you can see me pushing this huge bright-orange carrot in and out of my cunt, and my fingers are flicking my clitoris so fast they're practically a blur. Then you can hear me scream. It doesn't sound like me at all. I tried to keep my legs apart so that I could see myself having an orgasm, but I couldn't . . . although after it's all over I do open them up again. My labia minora are all red and my vagina's very wet and wide open.

"I learned a whole lot about myself from that session. I'd already *read* about sex, and how a woman's body was made, but to see it for yourself is something altogether different. Especially to see your own body responding and working like that.

"I learned not to be shy to touch myself and to stimulate myself. But more than anything else I learned that it was perfectly okay to be curious about myself. If I wanted to look up my cunt, then I could look up my cunt. If I wanted to know what it felt like to push a carrot up my cunt, then that was okay, too. When I first did this, (a) I didn't think I'd even be able to do it, and (b) I never thought that I'd be able to talk to anybody about it, especially so frankly, and using words like *cunt*. But I feel real happy with myself now, not just sexually but completely. I still feel that sex has a lot of mystery, but it's a mystery that I'm equipped to find out about. I know my body. Now I'm beginning to find out about my sexual desires and my sexual preferences, too. It never crossed my mind that a woman could have sexual preferences. As far as I knew, women just got laid. But I have a thing for making love in the shower, and I definitely like doing it when I'm fully dressed and Bernie's naked. And I like him touching me up in company, when nobody can see. We went around to his mother's house for coffee one morning, and we sat on the couch for almost a half-hour, just chatting, and all the time he had his finger up my cunt. What was even more of a turn-on, we'd made love just before we left, and so he was dabbling around in his own cum. I was sure that his mother would be able to smell it. *I* could; and her dog was going crazy for a sniff up my skirt.

"Seriously, though, I can't think of a better way for a girl to discover her own body than to make a video. I've watched mine four or five times, and I'm thinking of making another one. I might even make one of Bernie. That would be great bedtime viewing, don't you think?"

Before we continue, it's worth mentioning the G-spot. You may have heard about it or read about it. The G-spot is supposed to be the female equivalent of the male prostate gland. It's said to be located in the front wall of the vagina, 3 to 5 centimeters from the entrance to the vagina, and it's said to be sensitive to firm stimulation with the fingers or with a vibrator. Some sex-toy companies even sell a special G-spot vibrator, which has an upwardly curving end, so that a woman can insert it into her vagina and give herself extra pressure on the G-spot.

Stimulation of the G-spot is supposed to give

women an especially volcanic type of orgasm. One 27-year-old German housewife is quoted as saying: "I rubbed with both fingers on the front wall, right behind the vagina entrance, and suddenly I touched something quite different inside. At the same time, something strange happened: I got a wonderful feeling down below, while the spot I was rubbing swelled up. A hard nodule formed, which grew as big as a hazelnut. I rubbed and rubbed, experiencing such a feeling of happiness. And then it happened. At first I felt a remarkable warmth inside me, and shortly afterwards I had such a strong orgasm that I couldn't help arching and shouting out. At the same time I noticed I had wet all over the bed."

"Deep Orgasms"—True or False?

It's a little difficult to imagine a 27-year-old German housewife talking about "nodules," but there have been serious claims that a G-spot exists and that apart from being responsible for "deep" orgasms, it leads to female ejaculation—a flood of fluid that certainly isn't urine. In fact, many women are said to have been embarrassed by the copiousness of their wetness, and have sought their doctor's advice to stop it.

Despite the claims made for the G-spot, there is no physical evidence that such a gland exists, and common sexual sense should have made a couple of points immediately clear. The first is that any woman who takes time to stimulate the front of her vaginal wall is bound to become highly stimulated—mainly because she is already feeling aroused enough to want to do it.

The second is that, if a woman's lover stimulates her with his fingers in the special G-spot position recommended in some of the G-spot books and pamphlets I have studied, with two fingers curved deeply inside her vagina and the ball of his thumb pressed against the outside of her vulva in opposition to these two fingers, he will be applying firm, rhythmic, and steady pressure to her clitoris. The clitoris is not just a little pea on the outside of a woman's vulva; that's just the tip of the iceberg, the glans of the clitoris. The whole organ is buried beneath, and is (on average) about an inch long. It varies in shape from one woman to another—short and fat, tall and thin—just as women's labia vary. The so-called hazelnut is nothing more startling than the aroused clitoris felt from *inside* the body rather than outside.

It's hardly surprising that women have powerful and very satisfying orgasms from strong and determined stimulation of the clitoris, but the G-spot is a *technique* rather than an organ. I also find the idea of "female ejaculation" to be highly suspect. Sexologists have argued among themselves for years about where a woman's sexual wetness actually comes from. Some say Bartholin's glands (now largely discredited), some say Skene's glands (whose??), and the G-spot gang claim that she's got a completely new gland altogether.

A woman who is skillfully and thoughtfully aroused by a lover who is concerned about her pleasure and her eventual satisfaction will almost always become extremely wet—enough to account for the tales of soaking sheets and "female ejaculation."

I have nothing against the G-spot technique in principle. In fact, I welcome anything that gives men and women more intense sexual pleasure and inspires them to try to achieve it. But I think it only fair to tell you that there is no magic switch within a woman's vagina. Strong "earthquake" orgasms are achieved by a number of different factors—some of which will always be accidental. The right mood, the right man, the right moment. Something she saw, something she heard about, something she drank. All of these things can affect a woman's state of arousal, as well as her own sexual skill and the skill of the man with whom she's making love.

Another aspect of the G-spot theory that I dislike is the overemphasis placed on orgasm. Although orgasm is obviously desirable, and many women who *never* achieve it become depressed and frustrated, it is quite possible (and common) for a woman to enjoy making love and to feel satisfied afterward *without* having reached a climax.

As 35-year-old Cheryl, from Houston, Texas, told me, "There are times of the month, especially just before my period, when I find it very difficult to reach a climax. I can feel real horny, and I could make love all night if you wanted me to, or even if you didn't want me to. But I never reach a climax. I begin to feel it coming up inside of me, then it dies down again, and so it goes on. And I can go on for literally *hours*, enjoying every single minute of it, and the only thing that ever brings the proceedings to a close is my husband reaching *his* climax, and that's the end of that."

A large majority of women have the same difficulty—except that it isn't really a difficulty, it's just the natural cycle of mind and body. Understanding that it isn't always obligatory to reach a climax can ease a great deal of the tension that surrounds lovemaking—for both men and women. There are many times when men can't make it, either. They may be tired, they may have had too much to drink, they may be suffering from stress. The best attitude is not to worry about it. The very best sex is all about pleasure and satisfaction and achieving total closeness, and if you can do all of those things, you'll discover that climaxes aren't all that important.

Let's move on now to Greg, a 22-year-old heating engineer from Seattle, who agreed to try some sexual self-exploration with the aid of a video camcorder. Greg was the second of two brothers, and had what he calls a "pretty damn frank" sexual education. His mother was divorced when he was 10, and went through a number of casual relationships before she remarried eight years later. On several occasions, Greg and his brothers would spy on their mother while she was having sex, and so "I guess you could say that I'd seen it all by the time I was twelve."

All the same, he felt less confident about his own sex life. He had six or seven steady girlfriends, and slept with all of them, but somehow he always felt that he was missing something. "I feel like I'm all at sea when it comes to sex. Like I'm doing it, you know, but I don't know why. I get a kick out of it, but it's the same kick every time. It always leaves me feeling kind of empty. I've broken up with most of my girlfriends because I got bored. Now I'm in love, and I'm thinking of getting married, but I'm scared that Suzie's going to bore me, too. Or maybe it's *me* who's boring."

A great deal of Greg's sex problems could be attributed to his unstable family background, and his reluctance to commit himself emotionally to a deep relationship. In fact I talked to his fiancée Suzie, who complained that "he always seems to be holding some part of himself in reserve . . . like there's part of his personality that he doesn't want to share."

Many children of divorced or separated parents have difficulty forming close relationships—and when they do, they are statistically much more likely to commit themselves to the wrong partner than children from stable families, for the wrong reasons. It's understandable, but it's curable, especially if you make an effort to develop sexual confidence and sexual skill. Knowing how to give and receive sexual pleasure can have an extremely beneficial effect on other aspects of your personality and your emotional equilibrium. After all, peak-performance sex depends on dedicating yourself to your partner's enjoyment and excitement, while at the same time deriving the maximum possible pleasure for yourself.

Greg knew the basic facts of life. At least he knew that babies weren't found under gooseberry bushes. He knew about contraception and he knew about women's orgasms. But spying on his mother had seriously affected his view of how lovemaking should be carried out—and it was further evidence that, although it should always be frank and explicit, sex education should always be carefully graded according to a young person's emotional maturity. Greg, at the age of 10, had seen strangers forcefully humping his mother, some of them shouting obscenities, and his idea of lovemaking was a brief and violent encounter, with a great many dirty words thrown in.

No child of 10 can be expected to understand the forcefulness of lovemaking as it reaches its climax (he hadn't seen any of the courting or the foreplay . . . it was only the climaxes that had influenced him). Nor can he be expected to understand the part that "talking dirty" can play. Even the most prudish mothers can shout out "fuck me, fuck me!" while they're in the throes of lovemaking, but it isn't anybody's business except her lover's and her own. I don't believe that pornography has any harmful effect: in fact I believe that, for the most part, it's educational, stimulating, and provides many law-abiding and well-balanced people with fun, arousal, and well-deserved sexual release. But I don't believe in showing it to young people who are not mature enough to understand what they're looking at; and I do believe that parents and teachers should discuss it openly before young people are likely to come into contact with it, acknowledge its existence, and put it into the proper perspective. People who are offended by pornography shouldn't have it shoved in their faces: but people who enjoy it should be able to buy it without being treated like perverts or potential serial-killers.

This is Greg's report on how he explored himself sexually. "I chose an afternoon because I wanted to do it during daylight. I guess I felt there would be something more open about it if I did it in daylight. Besides, I have a small balcony where the sun comes in during the afternoon, and I could sit on the floor with the balcony door open, and rest the mirror against the frame, and get a real good view of myself.

"I Measured My Penis"

"I don't have a camcorder of my own so I rented a camcorder and a tripod from the photographic store. It was a pretty good one, state of the art. Well—if you're going to film the best equipment, you need the best equipment, right? I set up the tripod and the camcorder outside on the balcony and tested it a couple of times. Then I went to the bathroom and undressed and showered. It's strange, because I'm not naturally a nervous person, but I found that I had this knot in my stomach, like when you're taking an exam or something.

"I dried myself and went back to the open door. I sat down on the floor and opened up my legs. I already had half a hard-on. It was difficult for me to understand at first that there was all that much for me to look at. After all, a guy looks at his dong every day of the week, right; how can you miss it? Anyway, I did what you suggested and squeezed a little hand cream into the palm of my hand, and then slowly massaged my cock until I had a full hard-on.

"I think I have a reasonably big cock, yes. I measured it when it was fully hard, and it was just under 7 inches long, measured from the top. Seven inches long and 2½ inches around." [Penises generally vary in length from 5½ to 7 inches long, but very narrow girth—usually 2¾ inches to 3 inches.] "I was never circumcized because all of us were born at home, and our family doctor didn't care too much for circumcision. I think that girls like it when you're not circumcized . . . they like to roll back your foreskin and then roll it back again. I've heard it said that uncircumcized penises are less sensitive than circumcized penises; but then again I've also heard it said that circumcized penises are less sensitive than uncircumcized penises, because the head of your penis is always rubbing against your shorts or whatever and it gets used to being touched."

Of course there is no definitive way of telling whether men with circumcized penises are more or *less* sexually sensitive than men with uncircumcized penises. A certain amount of ribald and unscientific propaganda is put out by both sides. Masters and Johnson—in the sexual experiments they carried out in the laboratory—detected no difference in the speed with which circumcized or uncircumcized men reached a climax. My own feeling is that unless there is a religious or a prima facie medical reason for circumcision, then the foreskin should be left intact.

"The head of my cock is much more sensitive than the shaft, yes. I don't think some girls realize this. They don't understand that they can grip the shaft real hard, and that it's the head of the cock that likes all the tickling. Especially around the opening, and just below the opening. A girl can stroke you there with the tip of her finger and that's terrific. It's interesting, my cock is more sensitive underneath than it is on top, all the way down.

"I slowly rubbed my cock for a while, until a little clear juice appeared in the opening. It was only a couple of drops, but I massaged it around the head of my cock and it lubricated the whole thing. I didn't realize that this juice could have a few stray sperm in it . . . that'll teach me to be careful! I used the withdrawal method a couple of times . . . you know, pulling my cock out before I climaxed so that she wouldn't get pregnant. I didn't realize it was that much of a risk."

He also hadn't realized that this lubricating fluid contains chemicals that try to neutralize anything in a woman's vagina that might be potentially harmful to sperm, so it gives those stray sperm (and any subsequent sperm that escape during intercourse) a better chance of survival. Many condoms, on the other hand, apart from preventing sperm being ejaculated into the vagina, are treated with spermicide.

"I tried to make it a habit, wearing a condom. I can't say that I ever liked condoms, not ever—not even some of the weird ones we tried, with ridges and bumps and fringes. But I guess you have to face up to the risk of getting a girl pregnant and the risk of AIDS, and so you have to do it, amen. But I guess it would help if putting on a condom became more of a natural part of making love . . . more of a thing that men and women did together . . . if girls were taught at school to roll a rubber onto a guy's cock. They wouldn't have to use a real one, would they? I mean, they learn how to roll out pastry, don't they? And what's more useful?

"Now I did the technical bit, according to the books you gave me. I felt the two hard columns of flesh that made up the top part of my cock . . . what were they called? the *corposa cavernosa.* Then I felt the column underneath that makes up the glans and the underside of the shaft—here we are, the *corposum spongiosum.* So what happens is that these fill up with blood when I get turned on, but the blood vessels which allow the blood *out* again get closed off. So my cock was filled up with blood like a hard balloon.

"I found it interesting to see how a hard-on worked. The right frame of mind is definitely essential. I used to have a lot of instant hard-ons when I was about 14 and 15 years old. I could be sitting in a *math* lesson and I could have a hard-on. But these days I definitely have to feel like it. I can masturbate myself into a hard-on, but if I lose interest or lose my concentration, then my cock will just die down again. On the other hand, I can be lying in bed thinking sexy thoughts, and I can almost get to the point of bringing myself off without even touching my cock at all.

Making it Hard and Keeping it Hard

"I think a lot of girls don't really understand that if they break the mood, they can ruin a guy's concentration, and if they ruin his concentration, he can lose his hard-on. Also a guy needs to know that what he's doing to a girl is having some effect. You wouldn't believe the number of girls who just lie there while you're fondling their breasts and stroking their cunts and giving it all you've got, they literally just lie there and you don't even know if they're enjoying themselves or not. After a while you can think to yourself, what the hell am I doing, I might just as well go home and twiddle the knobs on my hi-fi. That's when you lose the hard-on . . . that's when you lose the mood. And of course *that's* when she says, 'what's the matter?' and you realize that she *was* getting turned on after all. The only problem was that she wasn't letting you know it.

"Just like the thoughts in your own mind can make your cock go up and down, the thoughts in your girlfriend's mind can make your cock go up and down. If she lets you know that she wants it, then she doesn't necessarily have to touch it . . . although I don't mind that, either. You know, making your cock go hard and keeping it hard, it's kind of like the Indian rope trick, mind over matter.

"After I'd felt the shaft of my cock, I felt my balls. You don't realize how complicated they are till you feel them. Most of the girls I've slept with have either been too rough with them, and squeezed them too hard, or else they've been scared of touching them at all. But a gentle kind of *holding* is good, especially when your cock is right up inside her. And some stroking, too, and some sucking . . . but not too hard.

"I carried on rubbing my cock, and my balls started to tighten and I began to feel that a climax was pretty close. So I stopped rubbing for a while, and relaxed, and a whole lot more of that clear juice ran out of the top of my cock. I used it to lubricate my thumb for the next exercise. I wasn't at all sure about this, but it sounded like something I ought to try.

"I lay on my back on the floor, with my legs drawn up. Then I gently pushed my lubricated thumb up my ass, as far as I could. At the same time I could stroke my balls with my fingers. I pressed my thumb against the front wall of my rectum, and rubbed it. I couldn't feel my prostate gland at first, but then I did, like a soft spongy object. I wasn't too sure that I liked the feeling, I've got to tell you. It was weird, like nothing I've felt before. But it definitely began to be sexual. The more I rubbed, the sexier I got, and I started to think sexy thoughts—you know, fantasies, like having two girls suck my cock at the same time, and slowly masturbating myself with all these naked girls watching me.

"Then before I knew it, I had this incredible sensation between my legs, and sperm poured out of me . . . I mean, it *poured*, rather than squirted. I lay back with sperm all over my stomach and I felt shattered. Shattered, but satisfied. If only more women knew they could do that to the men in their lives . . . well, there'd be a whole lot more smiles on a whole lot more faces."

It takes skill (and some manual strength) for a woman to be able to massage her lover's prostate gland in this way, and it is usually more successful as a masturbation technique than as a part of foreplay or lovemaking. A woman can use it, for instance, when she's unable to have intercourse herself, because of pregnancy or period, or when she simply doesn't feel like making love but is quite willing to give her lover some sexual satisfaction.

Even so, it's difficult for a woman to resist touching or rubbing her lover's penis during masturbation, and so the *pouring* effect will probably be lost in a typical climactic spasm.

The technique is interesting to know about, however, because it gives a man a feeling of what's going on inside his own body during sex. He can clench the muscles between his legs and greatly increase the speed and the intensity of his climax, because in effect he's massaging his prostate gland by muscular contraction alone. Any man can try this muscular clenching at any time . . . in fact, it's an excellent sexual exercise, and it's possible for a man to climax while sitting in an office chair by muscle-clenching alone, without even touching his penis.

She *Penetrates* Him

Just because a woman may find it difficult to locate and massage her lover's prostate gland, however, doesn't mean that she can't stimulate his anal region during lovemaking. The anus itself is rich in sensitive nerves, and simply by inserting the tip of her finger in his anus and gently tugging, a woman can highly stimulate her partner, greatly increasing the strength of his climax. Many men (if they would only admit it) also enjoy the insertion of a vibrator into their anus during lovemaking; and the use of a vibrator can give a woman a very erotic sense that *she's* penetrating his body at the same time that *he's* penetrating hers.

Many men, however, are inhibited about anal stimulation because they fear that it smacks of homosexuality. In actual fact, not nearly as many homosexuals practice anal intercourse as is commonly believed; and even those who *do* practice it surprisingly infrequently. Much more anal intercourse goes on between men and women; and there are literally scores of publications from Scandinavia and Holland (and indeed from the United States) that are devoted to nothing else.

But back to Greg. After completing his sexual self-exploration, he said, "I came out of it with the feeling that there was a whole lot more going on inside of me when I made love than I realized, and that I ought to make more of an effort to find out about the physical side of sex. I watched my video over and over, and I learned a lot about how my cock reacted and how I touched it to give myself the most stimulation.

"I also found that I wanted to know more about women's bodies, too. They're not just holes for men to stick their cocks into, although I guess a lot of men treat them that way. I'd say that it changed my attitude towards sex, yes. I don't feel that I know everything there is to know, the way I used to, just because I've slept with a few girls. I'm eager to find out more. But I also think that girls ought to be taught the same kind of thing. Like, how a man works, how to touch him, what turns him off, what turns him on.

"I feel more confident about marrying Suzie, I must say. In fact I can hardly wait. I've found out that sex is a whole galaxy out there—you know, just waiting for me to boldly go where no man has gone before."

You can use a camcorder at any time to check and recheck your sexual responses, or those of your partner, or both. Surprisingly—although most people normally become stilted and shy when they're being video-recorded, posing and grimacing and acting unnaturally—they seem to behave much more naturally when they're posing naked or masturbating or making love. One 35-year-old man from Philadelphia, remarked, "My wife would have been very reluctant to let me stand and stare at her while she was naked, or watch her fingering herself, or anything like that. But when I had the camcorder in front of my face, somehow it made it all different. She posed for it, she really played up to it. In the end she lay back on the bed and pulled open her pussy and said, "Get a going-in shot.' It's a pretty startling piece of video, I can tell you. The camcorder zooms right toward her open pussy, and then she actually took the lens up inside of her. You can see every detail of her pussy, pin-sharp. You never saw such a close-up. Then it's all darkness."

Joan, a 28-year-old secretary from Flint, Michigan, had a similar close-up of her live-in lover Billy, 30: "The head of his cock fills up the entire screen, bobbing around because he's jerking himself off. Then you see his sperm shooting out, and it actually hits the lens and slides down."

9

Super-Stimulation

Another advantage of video-recording your sex life is that it enables you to look at yourself as your lover sees you—not just a mirror-image. And it enables you to look at your sexual performance much more objectively; in other words, you can watch yourself posing or masturbating or making love at a time when you're no longer sexually aroused, and your perception of what you're doing and how you're doing it isn't colored by your stimulated state of mind.

This is how 41-year-old Dean and his 37-year-old wife Maria, from Los Angeles, used a camcorder to analyze their sexual problems, which were preventing them from making any progress toward peak-performance sex.

"As you know, Maria and I had been having sexual problems on and off for five or six years. She found it more and more difficult to reach an orgasm, and I began to think that either I was doing something wrong; or that maybe our lovemaking was just becoming too routine; or that maybe I simply didn't turn her on anymore.

"Because of that, I started to doubt my sexual ability, and I began to suffer from bouts of impotence. I began to dread going to bed because I never knew whether I ought to try making love to Maria or not, or even if I did, whether I would be able to manage it. There can't be many worse feelings in this world than getting your wife all turned on and ready to go, and then finding that you can't get a hard-on. You look down at that cock and you *will* it to go hard, but it seems like you can't even feel it. It's like a useless dingle-dangle that's no good for nothing.

"Anyway, we agreed to try video-recording ourselves, even though we weren't even sure that we'd be able to make it. Fortunately, the whole idea of making the recording was quite a turn-on for both of us, so Maria was quite responsive and I got that precious erection. We filmed ourselves making love three times, in three different positions."

The video shows Dean and Maria's bedroom, and their king-sized bed. Maria appears in the picture first: she's a dark-haired, slightly Hispanic-looking woman with high cheekbones and a full, sensual mouth. She is a little heavy-hipped, and her stomach is rounded from childbearing, but she has large firm breasts and very smooth, silky skin. She lies on the bed naked, waiting for Dean, who appears shortly afterward, with the beginnings of an erection.

Dean is a stocky man of average height, with iron-gray hair and a firm jawline. He is at least 30 pounds overweight, and sports a beer belly. ("Yes . . . as you can see there, I like an occasional six-pack.") He climbs on to the bed next to Maria, props himself up on one elbow, and starts to kiss her and caress her breasts. His penis hardens and rises against her thigh. She reaches across and strokes it up and down. Things appear to be going reasonably well.

Suddenly, however, Dean climbs on top of Maria, opens her thighs, and pushes himself into her. They begin to move quickly up and down in the rhythms of intercourse, although not very fluidly. No dancing, in other words. It's very noticeable that Dean's back is quite straight, and that he is keeping himself well propped up. He fucks Maria very quickly and jerkily, and after only three minutes he ejaculates, and their lovemaking is over. He climbs off her and kisses her.

The second time, he makes love to her from the side. Again, he kisses her, caresses her breasts, and then suddenly penetrates her. He lifts her left thigh so that he can penetrate her as deeply as possible, and keeps his hand under her knee to support her upraised leg throughout the act of intercourse. He starts off fucking her very fast and hard, then seems to run out of energy, and pauses. After a while he starts again, quick bursts of fucking. Then he tires and withdraws without ejaculating.

The third time, he makes love to her from behind. She is lying on her side with her legs drawn up. He kisses her back, and puts his hand around her and gently squeezes her left breast. Then he penetrates her, although now he seems to angle his upper body away from her. He makes love to her very slowly and it takes him nearly ten minutes to climax. During all of this time Maria shows no visible response to what he is doing to her.

The fascinating part about this video experiment was that Dean had said that, "Our sex life was great . . . up until five or six years ago, we were really hot stuff in bed. We did everything, all the positions. We still do. But somehow the fire just went out of it. Don't ask me why." Even Maria said, "Our sex life was fine. We were very close, everything was fine. Dean was a very considerate lover."

It was quite obvious from the video, however, that Dean had been a way below-average lover, in terms of his sexual skills. He hadn't understood Maria's need to be caressed and aroused before intercourse began—nor her need to be continuously stimulated during the act of love. As she grew older, and the years made them sexually more familiar to each other, she needed much more intensive physical stimulation. Not only that, she needed to be reassured that she was still attractive, still sexy, and that Dean wasn't simply using her body in order to satisfy his occasional feelings of sexual tension.

He hadn't realized that she needed to be treated like a woman.

He Questioned His Virility

To be fair, Dean hadn't had the necessary sexual education or the sexual experience to deal with their problem—and neither had Maria. It was quite some time, in fact, before they realized that it *was* a problem, and by then it was almost too late to correct it. Maria's inability to reach an orgasm and Dean's repeated bouts of impotence had become two interlocking vicious circles.

But with the aid of the videotape they were able to see and assess the problem for themselves—comparatively objectively—and at a time when neither of them was sexually aroused or was *trying* to become sexually aroused.

After the birth of their last child, Maria had become less interested in sex for a time, and even when her sexual appetite began to return, she found it more difficult to reach an orgasm than she had before the child was born—not an uncommon phenomenon. During those months when Maria had lost interest, Dean began to question his sexual attractiveness and his virility and had suffered his first bouts of impotence. It's quite difficult to sustain an erection when your partner obviously couldn't care less whether you've got one or not—and, in fact, would rather you hadn't.

By the time Maria's sexual interest had revived, Dean was so anxious and self-conscious about achieving and sustaining an erection that—every time he got one—he made sure that he penetrated Maria as quickly as possible, and climaxed as quickly as possible, before his erection disappeared. By the time he had finished, Maria was hardly stimulated at all, and nowhere near orgasm. Dean could tell, of course, that she was disappointed and frustrated, and this made him even *more* anxious about sex, and even *less* likely to achieve a full and lasting erection.

Both Dean and Maria neglected their physical well-being. If their sex life was such a failure, there seemed to be no reason for either of them to make an effort to look sexy and attractive. Maria started smoking; Dean started drinking quite heavily, put on weight, and became sluggish and unfit.

The video clearly showed Dean's lack of stamina. It also showed that because his stomach protruded, when he wanted to achieve maximum penetration of his penis he had to position himself in such a way that his pubic bone gave Maria very little clitoral pressure—not that this pressure, in itself, would have been sufficient to stimulate her to orgasm.

Still using the video to monitor their progress, I recommended that the next time Dean took Maria to bed, he forget about getting an erection. I told him not to worry about it. Instead, he should concern himself with making Maria come. He should kiss her, caress her, fondle her breasts and her nipples—he should put every ounce of his being into making her feel sexually excited. He should caress and stimulate her clitoris, finger-fuck her vagina, and then go down on her and give her a long and luxurious tonguing.

Only when he had managed consistently to give Maria a satisfying orgasm should he start to concern himself with his own stimulation, and by that time he didn't need to. He was regularly achieving erections—long-lasting erections.

Maria needed more flirtation, more foreplay, more caresses, more of everything. When he was making love to her, Dean had to ensure that she was being properly and consistently aroused. This meant stimulating her clitoris with his fingers during intercourse, and *continuing* to stimulate it even after his own climax, to make sure that she had a climax, too.

I also suggested a diet and exercise program. Nothing too strenuous: I didn't expect him to run an Olympic marathon. But every lover has a duty to be sound enough of wind and limb to be able to make love creatively and energetically without collapsing in a gasping heap.

Maria, because she was more sexually satisfied, began to respond, which helped to restoke the fire of their (nearly extinguished) sexual relationship.

I can't recommend strongly enough that you use a camcorder to try your own sexual self-analysis. When you're viewing, here are some of the common sexual problems to be aware of:

1. Location: Is your bedroom comfortable, romantic, and secure from interruption? It doesn't have to be a palace, as long as it's nicely decorated and looks like a place for love.

2. Physical appearance: Look at yourself on the screen. Do you think you *look* attractive? Is your hair washed, your teeth bright, your nails clipped? Are you shaved and perfumed? You don't *always* have to look like this when

you make love, but good hygiene shows sexual consideration.

3. Kissing: Is there any? Who appears to want it the most? Whose tongue is in whose mouth? Does the kissing stop when the intercourse begins?

4. Foreplay: Does his hand go directly to her vagina? Does he forget about her breasts altogether (it's surprising how many men do!)? Is there any kissing and caressing of any part of the anatomy apart from breasts and genitalia?

5. Oral stimulation: Does she kiss his penis? If so, how does she do with it? With relish, or as a hurried duty? Does he lick her vulva?

6. Penetration: Are you both comfortable? Are you both *ready*? Are you acting in unison or is the man penetrating his partner without regard for the degree of her arousal? Does she assist him in sliding his penis into her?

7. Intercourse: Does the position look comfortable? Did it *feel* comfortable? Do your two bodies look as if they're dancing or fighting, or joggling backward and forward on a rollercoaster? Is there an obvious and steadily building rhythm? Is the man doing anything to arouse his partner (fondling her breasts, clitoris, or both)?

8. Climax: Does it look as if any attempt is being made by either or both of you to climax together—or at least, reasonably close?

9. Climax II: Who climaxes first—and does this person then make an effort to make sure that the partner climaxes, too (with enthusiasm, that is, not as a chore!)?

10. Après sex: Is there an obvious air of satisfaction, contentment, and a mutual display of

affection, including lingering kisses and gentle and intimate caresses?

11. Variations: Note any sexual variations (such as bondage, erotic dressing, etc.), and ask each other how much of a turn-on it really was, and whether you *both* really enjoyed it.

10

His Peak-Performance Body

It's a startling thought, but most men know far more about the workings of their automobile engines than they do about the workings of their own sexual organs. And this is despite the fact that they expect to get many years of happiness, well-being, and satisfaction from their sexual organs—without (we hope) a single repair.

Women—try this test on the man in your life: ask him (a) how fuel injection works; then (b) how male ejaculation works. I'll bet you 10 to 1 that he can answer (a) a great deal more knowledgeably than (b).

It's critical for peak-performance sex that a man understands what's happening inside his own body during sex. Only then can he maximize the stimulation that he is able to give to the woman in his life; and only then can he experience the intense erotic sensations that peak-performance sex can offer.

Once you have achieved peak-performance sex—once you have realized what overwhelming sexual pleasure you are able both to give and to receive—you will look back at the way you're making love today and realize that, pleasurable though it is, it gave you only *half* the excitement, only *half* the satisfaction.

As we've seen from the previous chapter, the first step in reaching your sexual peak is to familiarize yourself with your own body, and to understand that sexual well-being starts with self-knowledge and self-confidence. By the time you have examined and stimulated yourself, you should feel comfortable about handling and massaging and looking at your own sexual organs without embarrassment or guilt. *Nothing that you do to yourself sexually (provided it causes no physical injury) can possibly be wrong*.

I have had many men of all ages write me to say: "I feel ashamed and guilty because I masturbate. I've tried to break the habit time and time again, but I just can't stop. I quit smoking, how come I can't quit jerking myself off?"

The guiltiest men are those who continue to masturbate after they have involved themselves in a long-term sexual relationship, or marriage. "My wife would go crazy if she knew that, when she goes out shopping, I take out all of these pornographic magazines and spend half an hour masturbating all over them. But there's nothing wrong with our sex life. In fact our sex life is excellent."

These men should stop feeling guilty as of now. Just as there is absolutely nothing wrong with young boys masturbating, there is nothing wrong with grown men masturbating either—even married men— and a huge proportion do. It doesn't mean that they're sexually dissatisfied with their partners. It simply means that they're indulging themselves in sexual fantasies which (for one reason or another) they feel unwilling or unable to share.

These fantasies are usually their most extreme sexual thoughts. George, a 32-year-old science teacher from Pittsburgh, said, "I have fantasies during masturbation that even make *me* blush when I think about them afterwards. I fantasize that a whole lot of my young girl students grab hold of me and strip me and do every conceivable thing to me . . . like three of them sucking my cock at once. I've never been attracted to any of my students and I wouldn't dream of abusing my position of trust . . . but there it is, that's the fantasy, and that's the first time I've told anybody, including my wife."

It's very difficult for any man brought up with a traditional view of sex and marriage to explain his darkest and most erotic fantasies to his partner—and it's not always desirable or necessary that he should. All of us keep some extreme self-stimuli locked in the back of our minds, to be brought out only at moments of intense sexual arousal. When those moments of intense sexual arousal are over, it's probably appropriate that those stimuli are locked up once again. In the light of day, they can seem perverse—even threatening—and they may introduce confusion and uncertainty into a sexual relationship, which may be quite healthy.

For instance, 34-year-old Davina, a fashion-store buyer from Fort Worth, Texas, wrote: "When I am feeling very aroused, I have what I call my dungeon fantasy. My boyfriend Ned is completely naked and chained to the wall of this dungeon. I am dressed in a tight black leather bra which has holes in the front for my nipples to poke through, and tight black leather shorts with an open crotch. I wear studded wristbands and black leather thigh-boots with stiletto heels. I have a leather braided whip and as I get more excited I whip Ned's shoulders and chest until it's all striped with red. He's covered in sweat and his erection is gigantic. I whip his penis again and again, and it bobs up and down with every whipping, until he finally shoots out his sperm. I have never mentioned this fantasy to Ned and I don't think that I ever will. I would not actually like to whip him like that, although I am quite aggressive in bed (e.g., I like to bite and scratch and I do like leather skirts and shorts). But I would like to know if there is anything wrong in having such a fantasy and also whether I am holding something back by not telling Ned about it. You have always said that couples ought to be totally honest and open in their sexual relationships and somehow I feel that with this dungeon fantasy (and some others) I am holding something back."

Skintight Leather and Shiny Rubber

In many respects, Davina answered her own question. She didn't think that it was necessary for her to tell her boyfriend about her fantasy, simply because it would have made him feel that she was unfulfilled, and that in order to satisfy her completely, he ought to act it out for real. *There is no sexual or emotional necessity to act fantasies out.* Quite often, when couples *do* try to play out their fantasies, they turn out to be a crushing disappointment. It's one thing to fantasize about whipping, for example. In reality, of course, it's extremely painful. It's one thing to fantasize about skintight leather and shiny rubber. In reality, leather can be hot and pungent and uncomfortable, and rubberware somehow never looks as erotic in reality as it does in the imagination.

Rob, 51, an accountant from Chicago, had an occasional fantasy about coming home unexpectedly and finding his wife having sex with a huge dog. "This image kind of flashes into my mind's eye when I'm very close to coming. I open the bedroom door and she's naked on the bed, on all fours, and this massive Dalmatian has mounted her. She's moaning out loud, and her breasts are swaying as the dog fucks her. I can see its black cock going in and out of her pink cunt as clearly as if it were real. Black and pink. Animal and human. That's all: that's the sum total of the fantasy. When I repeat it now, in this office, it seems disgusting. I wouldn't tell Hattie about it, no way. She'd think I was some kind of certifiable pervert. I love her desperately, after twenty-six years of happy marriage. She's good in bed. I'd like to make love a little more frequently than we do, but who wouldn't? I only strayed once, when she was pregnant with our second child, but it didn't mean anything and it finished after two or three weeks and I didn't tell her about *that*, either."

So what are the ground rules for telling or *not* telling your sexual fantasies? Generally speaking, your sexual relationship will be closer and more creative if you *do* discuss all of your most vivid fantasies. But this is a time when only you can be the judge of how your partner will react to what you have to say. Some women are appalled when their lovers tell them what's been going on in their heads during lovemaking. Most women who react this way are almost always lacking in sexual self-confidence, and they interpret their lover's fantasy as an unfulfilled need that *they* will now be obliged to satisfy.

It's not just women who feel this way. Plenty of men react with suspicion and hostility when they discover *women's* fantasies. They feel jealous and threatened by the men who have been courting their wives and girlfriends inside their minds—all those athletes and movie stars and Chippendales dancers.

But you should never forget that a fantasy is only a fantasy: it's an imaginary stimulus created in the mind. Even if you fantasize about having sex with your secretary, two hundred naked virgins, and two donkeys, what goes on in your mind has no material substance and (regardless of what Jimmy Carter once said about committing adultery in his mind) it doesn't necessarily mean that your sexual relationship is in any way lacking.

And whatever you're fantasizing about, you're using that fantasy to stimulate yourself, and the more you're stimulated, the better you'll be at stimulating your lover. So fantasizing can hardly be described as unfaithfulness.

Telling everything is still (to my mind) the best way to handle your fantasies. If you're both really open about it, and agree beforehand that no matter how kinky or wild your fantasies may turn out to be, you're going to accept them for what they are, which is simply fantasies—then you can have terrific fun describing them, and they may give you some unusual erotic ideas that can improve and enliven your sex life.

Here's Rita, 26, a flight attendant from St. Louis: "Jud and I talked about our sexual fantasies one evening. We'd been out to dinner with some good friends, and we'd been drinking wine, and we felt real mellow. We lay on cushions in the living room, next to the fire, and I asked Jud if he liked Laura (that's one of our friends) enough to make love to her. He said frankly that he'd fantasized about taking both of us to bed, Laura *and* me. I was kind of upset at first, but then he said, 'Don't tell me *you* never had any fantasies.' So we agreed that we would take it in turns to tell our pet fantasies. We rolled a die to see who kicked off first.

"I've Had Fantasies of Two or Three Men"

"It turned out it was me first. Just my luck! I had to tell Jud about my best-favorite fantasy, which I'd had for about six or seven months ever since I watched a bodybuilding contest on TV. I fantasized that there were all these muscular men going in for this contest, and it was my job to oil them ready for the show. For some reason I had to be naked as well. So I was in this locker room with about a dozen handsome men with hard bulging chests and narrow waists—all of them wearing these tiny satin posing shorts and nothing else. I rubbed oil all over their chests and their backs. I rubbed my breasts up against them and they liked that. I could almost feel the hard rows of muscles in their stomachs. Then I oiled my hands and slid them down the back of their shorts. I love men's bottoms when they're all rounded and hard and small. I could squeeze these guys' asses, and slid my oily fingers in between the cheeks of their ass and massage their assholes. Then I slid my hands around to the front, inside their satin shorts, and massaged their balls and their cocks with oil. Their balls and their cocks were completely hairless, I remember reading in a magazine how bodybuilders shaved . . . it must have stuck in my mind! Massaging them was like massaging a big hard sculpture . . . in my fantasy they all had huge twelve-inch cocks that I could hardly get my hands around.

"Anyway, I pulled down one man's shorts at the front, exposing his cock, and then I did the same to another, and I massaged two cocks at once, one in each hand. While I was doing it, a third man came up behind me and took hold of my hips, and pushed his enormous twelve-inch cock right up me. So I was rubbing two huge cocks, and being fucked at the same time. I could close my eyes, and Jud's cock sliding in and out of me could be this body-builder's cock, too . . . it was like a dream only it was real, too.

"I've had this fantasy maybe six or seven times, but there's never any finish to it. By the time I've thought about rubbing two cocks, I'm pretty close to coming myself . . . so somewhere in fantasy-land, there must be a whole lot of very frustrated bodybuilders!

"But the interesting thing is that I never see any of these guys' faces. I mean, I know they're hand-some, but that's it. They're just bodies and cocks . . . they're not men that I know. And when I've had fantasies about two or three men taking me to bed at once . . . they're not really anybody real at all. If you want the absolute honest truth, I'd love to go to bed with two or three men at once, but they'd all have to be Jud.

"Jud was a little upset at first when he heard about my fantasies, but when he realized that I didn't really want anybody else but him, he calmed down. In fact he got into the spirit of it, and told me a whole lot of *his* fantasies that I don't think he would have told me before. We did try a couple of things that we'd been fantasizing about. One was, Jud let me shave off all his pubic hair that Saturday afternoon, and massage his cock with oil. That was amazing . . . I told all my girlfriends about that. To feel a man's cock and balls completely smooth, to slide your hand up and down this warm, hard shaft, and all around his testicles, and it's all completely smooth, bare skin . . . there's nothing like it. In fact Jud's decided to stay that way . . . he says that once you've made love to a woman with no pubic hair, going back to it is almost as bad as wearing a condom. I sure don't mind, I love him that way. I can see everything he's got, and it's great for oral sex. I can take his whole cock into my mouth without choking on a bird's nest.

"Jud had a very weird fantasy about having a naked girl at work, who would kneel beneath his desk and suck his cock while he was working. I haven't done that yet, but I think it might be very exciting to try. The only trouble is, Jud's desk doesn't have a modesty screen . . . so everybody would see what was going on. We did try out one of his fantasies, though. He blindfolded me and then he undressed me completely, and led me out into the backyard, in the rain. He led me around and around until I didn't know where I was—then he made me lie down in the wet grass, and he touched me and massaged me all over with his cock. Then he climbed on top of me and fucked me. It was good, as a matter of fact, it was amazing. It was raining real hard, and thundering, and both of us were dripping, but the rain was warm, and right then I don't think I could have cared if it was or not."

You'll notice from Rita's account of her fantasy-sharing with Jud that they chose to enact only those parts of their fantasies that were both *possible* and *mutually enjoyable*. Some strong sexual fantasies may be possible to act out, but not mutually enjoyable (e.g., watching your wife having intercourse with a Dalmatian). You will have to use your own discretion.

A persistent sexual fantasy can mean that you have a strong sexual desire that remains frustrated. Be honest with yourself: is there something that you would like to do with your lover or which you would like your lover to do to you—something that you would *really* enjoy, something that you know would excite you—which you haven't had the nerve to tell her about?

That's when you have to put your courage to the test and tell your lover what you have been fantasizing about. Achieving peak-performance sex is all about taking your desires and your physical abilities to the very limit, and you can't possibly do that if there is always some unfulfilled urge in the back of your mind.

It often surprises me how reticent some lovers are about talking to each other about sex. They may have been sharing the same bed for years. They may have brought up children together. Yet they can never quite find the words or the courage to tell their partner that—for example—they would like to make love outdoors, or that they would like their partner to dress in erotic underwear, or try out sex toys, or watch sex videos together.

And many lovers simply *never* discuss their sexual fantasies. For fear of what? For fear of embarrassment? For fear of appearing to be a pervert, or a nymphomaniac? For fear of appearing dissatisfied?

Neither of you has anything to fear from your fantasies. They are nothing more than your mind's way of helping to arouse you. They are the means by which your imagination expresses your sexual excitement. In fact many therapists agree that the more extreme your fantasies, the more flattered your lover should be. Your fantasies are a full-color illustration of just how much he or she turns you on.

Just like Jud and Rita, you don't necessarily need to play out your fantasy to the hilt—or even at all. Sometimes it's enough of a turn-on simply to *talk* about it together. Michael, a 39-year-old technician from Seattle, had fantasized for years about taking his wife shopping dressed in nothing but a red rubber garter belt with red rubber stockings, and a red rubber raincoat to cover her. Eventually, one evening, he confessed his fantasy, expecting her to be shocked—or at the very least, disturbed. Far from it. Not only was she not shocked, but she discussed it with him, and actually embroidered the fantasy with erotic fantasies of her own. "Jane said she would have to have a long split up the back of the coat, so that I could slip my hand inside while we were walking around the store."

Michael's wife was not only understanding and appreciative about his fantasy, she ordered some rubber wear from a mail-order catalog. When he came home from work one evening, "she opened the door wearing red rubber panties and red rubber stockings, and she said, 'Well now, what do you think?' What did I think? I thought the top of my head was going to blow off."

Jane remarked that, "Rubber did nothing for me at all. I never understood why it turned Michael on so much, and I don't suppose I ever will. But I've accepted the fact that it *does*, whether I like it or not . . . just like it must turn a whole lot of people on, otherwise they wouldn't bother to make the garments, would they? And I think I'd be a pretty mean, uncaring wife if I didn't make the effort to wear one or two things that turn my husband on so much. It turns me on just to see how much I turn *him* on."

I've described the workings of the male sexual organs in considerable detail in previous books, especially in the chapters on mutual sexual discovery in *How to Make Love Six Nights a Week*. But now let's concentrate not only on a man's physical parts and how they work, but how they're *controlled* and how (as far as humanly possible) they can be trained to work better.

Just as modern automobiles depend not only on

well-tuned engines and well-constructed bodies, they rely on computers to sense the conditions around them and to alter the car's various functions (fuel injection, brakes, suspension) to give the machine a more responsive performance.

Brilliant Sex
Happens Inside Your Head

Similarly, a man's sexual skill depends not only on his physical fitness and his understanding of the mechanics of making love, it depends on his thinking and on his mental attitude—which can be trained just as much as his body, if not more.

Peak-performance sex is 10 percent physical ability, 20 percent knowledge and experience, and 60 percent mental control. There's no getting away from it, which is why I discussed sexual fantasy at some length; brilliant sex doesn't happen between your legs, it happens inside your head. You can be the very best lover that your partner has ever known, provided you are motivated.

Let's look now at the parts that make up a man's sexual organs, and see what *both* he and his lover can do to improve his skills.

As we saw during the sexual self-examinations, the obvious parts of the male sex organs are the penis and the testes. The head of the penis is called the *glans* and is rich with touch receptors, particularly where it joins the shaft of the penis, and particularly underneath, close to the opening (or, more scientifically, the urethral orifice). The glans is part of the *corposum spongiosum*, one of three columns of spongy tissue that fills up with blood during sexual arousal and stiffens the penis. The other two columns—the *corposa cavernosa*—are on the upper side, and are attached to the pelvic bone.

A man's penis becomes erect for many reasons. It's an automatic action brought about by nervous signals from the spinal column. But a whole variety of different stimuli can set these signals off, and not all of these stimuli are controllable. An erection could be triggered by the sight of a naked woman, or the sight of a *picture* of a naked woman, or by suggestive conversation, or by the anticipation of making love, or by direct touch.

Conscious thought, however, plays the major part in bringing about an erection. If a man can train himself to think stimulating thoughts *and to maintain his concentration*, he will stand a far better chance of achieving and sustaining a full and hard erection.

Conscious thought alone cannot necessarily bring about an erection. A man cannot simply stare at his penis and will it to rise (we wish!). But what he *can* do is radically improve his chances of getting it up and keeping it up once it's risen.

Here are some points to remember:

1. Don't be anxious. When you make love, don't worry whether you've got an erection or not, or whether you're going to be able to make it. Throughout recorded history, the onus has always been on men to produce the erection that makes sex possible, and the fact is that it hasn't always been possible. You don't prove or disprove anything about your virility by not getting an erection. So don't worry, and above all, don't *panic* (that will only make you feel worse), and don't get angry. Women understand that men occasionally can't get it up, but they tend to feel uncomfortable with men who occasionally can't get it up and then start throwing the bedroom furniture around in frustration.

2. Don't think about your erection, think about

pleasing your partner. Tell yourself, 'I'm going to make this girl feel like the universe has just exploded. So don't concentrate on your own petty concerns, concentrate on *her*, particularly the parts you like best—her mouth, and her breasts, and how soft and smooth and warm she is.

3. If you don't get an immediate erection, involve your partner in helping you to get one. Don't make excuses. Don't apologize. It's not your fault (unless you drank a fifth of Jack Daniel's before you went to bed). Above all, don't be shy about showing her your soft penis, or letting her fondle it. She'll be very pleased when she eventually coaxes it to rise. Just as it's *your* job to stimulate her in preparation for intercourse, it's *her* job to do the same to you. This is a moment when oral sex can be particularly effective. As 23-year-old Joanna, an artist from Sausalito, California, said: "Secretly I like it when my boyfriend can't get it on. I make him lie back on the bed and I kiss his cock and flop it around a bit, from side to side. Then I put the whole thing in my mouth, most of his balls and all. I gently suck it, and gradually I can feel it swelling in my mouth. That's such a turn-on. It gets bigger and bigger until I can't get it all in my mouth anymore, and then he's ready to go, no problem."

4. If you've had difficulty in attaining an erection, and you then manage to get one, don't destroy it by rushing to put it inside her before it disappears. This will only increase your anxiety and increase the chances of you losing it again—or of ejaculating prematurely and without much sense of pleasure. Climaxing too soon is itself a form of impotence. Take it slow, continue to think about giving her all the pleasure you can. Try kissing her breasts and then going down on her and kissing and licking her vulva. As you lick her, relish the taste of her, and

think about all of the things that excite you. Riffle through all of your favorite fantasies.

5. Rhythmically flex your perineal muscle (that muscle between your legs), and grip your penis hard in your hand, tugging down slightly on the skin of the shaft so that you stimulate the nerve receptors around the glans. You can do this while still kissing and caressing your lover with your other hand. Or she might even do it for you.

6. Use your penis to massage her breasts and her nipples. Show her how her erect nipple will just fit into the lubricated hole in the end of your penis. Slide your penis into her underarm; press it against her cheek; wrap her hair around it. Use it: it's part of you, and it's not meant just for intercourse.

7. When you *do* penetrate her, you may have no difficulty in maintaining an erection, but if you *do*, choose a position that affords you the maximum friction of penis against vagina. The straightforward man-on-top missionary position can be quite good for this (provided she doesn't spread her legs too wide), and you keep up a very relaxed, rhythmical rocking motion, penetrating as deep as you can. Otherwise, the side position is good, with her inner leg just resting on top of yours. You can reach around and draw her outer thigh toward you, thus virtually squeezing her legs together, and tightening the grip of her vagina on your penis. You can also moisten one finger with her vaginal juices and slide it into her anus, and stimulate your penis with your own finger through the thin skin that separates her vagina from her rectum.

The Secret
of Two *Male Climaxes*

8. After you have climaxed, you can increase your chance of being able to make it a second time if you *keep your penis inside her vagina*. Loss of erection or 103 *detumescence* occurs in two stages—first, when the penis shrinks from full erection to about 1½ times the size of the normal soft organ; second, a return to normal size.

After your climax, the previously stimulating sensation of rubbing your penis inside her vagina will now feel uncomfortable, and you won't want to continue making love. But if you lie still with your penis still inside her vagina, and continue to caress her and to think erotic thoughts, you will often find that your penis remains semierect, and that after about five minutes you will begin to harden, and feel like making some tentative thrusting movements again. If you take it easy, and keep your mind on arousing thoughts, you should be able to reach a second climax—I have occasionally heard of a third.

If you involve yourself in any action or movement involving the conscious mind, however, your penis will return to its normal size almost immediately. If you get up and walk around, if you urinate, if you reach for a cigarette, you will lose it.

I cannot emphasize strongly enough the importance of concentration in achieving skillful and satisfying loving. You can train yourself to concentrate when you drive. You can train yourself to concentrate when you play music or hit a golf ball or play a computer game. So why can't you train yourself to concentrate when you make love? *Concentrate*—use all of your knowledge and all of your experience and every single scrap of erotic advice and information you've ever been given. This sexual single-mindedness is the so-called secret of being a great lover. When he's making love, a great lover thinks only about arousing the woman in his arms, by any means possible, and about how much she excites him in return. Concentration is what makes a great lover's lovemaking electric and everybody else's lovemaking ordinary. From the moment he first sets eyes on a woman to the moment that he brings her to a stunning and satisfying orgasm, a great lover gives her the impression that he thinks and cares only about making her feel special.

Concentration is also the secret of what we might call good penis management. If you think lovemaking, if you think sex, your thoughts will be expressed in terms of a solid and lasting and very satisfying erection.

I'm not suggesting that it's always easy to concentrate only on sex. Most of us have to work and pay bills and suffer the stresses and strains of a modern, civilized existence. Stress of any kind can drastically affect a man's sexual performance—as can fatigue, or alcohol, or even doubts about his social status.

But the effects of stress on a man's sexual life can almost always be overcome by self-analysis. You know yourself better than anybody else: what could possibly be affecting your sexual performance? The answer may not always be glaringly obvious. I talked to a 45-year-old marine biologist in San Diego, who had been unable to achieve an erection for more than six months, and was beginning to despair. It turned out that he was very worried about the health and safety of several dolphins in his care, and his concern was revealing itself in his lack of sexual response. Once he had recognized the source of his anxiety, he was able to overcome it in a short time, and within a few days his sex life had returned almost to normal.

I can almost hear you saying "*dolphins*?" but the truth is that the anxiety that affects your sexual capability isn't necessarily connected in any way with your love life. So when you're analyzing your own sexual difficulties, don't restrict your investigations to the bedroom, or even to your lover and your family. Any ongoing anxiety can directly affect the performance of your penis—from stress at work to concerns about moving or going on vacation.

Vacations are always supposed to improve your sex life, but it's startling how many couples find that the high anxiety of packing and traveling and making a purposeful effort to relax and enjoy themselves is actually a severe downer when it comes to their lovemaking. Many couples report that they make love "considerably less frequently" on vacation, and I have come across a large proportion who say that they don't make love at all on vacation.

Again, it's a problem of loss of concentration. We can be easily distracted by unfamiliar surroundings, and any distraction can cause a man's penis to subside.

Phil, 39, a realtor from Darien, Connecticut, told me: "All of a sudden I found that I wasn't able to get completely hard. I could just about manage to make love to Sylvia, but it wasn't at all satisfactory. My penis was semisoft and didn't give her the feeling she needed. I couldn't understand what the problem was. I was fit, I didn't drink. I *felt* like making love. It took me a long time to work out what was wrong with me. The value of local property was falling, and I was anxious about offloading some of our larger houses. It seems like my penis was getting depressed in sympathy with the housing market."

Let's take a look at what a male sexual climax actually *is*—how it works, and what both a man and his lover can do to wring the last ounce of pleasure and performance out of that climax.

The male sexual climax includes many of the same physical reactions that occur during the female orgasm—with obvious specific differences, because of the bodily dissimilarities between men and women. For instance, during his climax, a man rarely experiences what we call *carpopedal spasm*, the involuntary contraction of the muscles in the feet during orgasm, which literally causes women's toes to curl (although some men *do* experience this response when they are lying on their backs with their lovers on top of them).

Before his climax, too, a man's penis secretes a few droplets of clear fluid, which act as a lubricant and also chemically prepare his lover's vagina for the ejaculation of sperm. As we said earlier, this fluid can contain viable sperms, so a man is capable of impregnating a woman even if he doesn't climax into her vagina—in fact, even if he doesn't climax at all. So be warned: use some protection.

This clear fluid is produced by the Cowper's glands, located deep in the base of the penis, just below the prostate gland. There is no particular sensation associated with its emission (in other words, a man can't feel it coming out), but more of it seems to be produced during intercourse than during masturbation or oral sex. This is because, during intercourse, a man is usually doing his best to hold back his climax, whereas he is usually trying to climax as quickly as possible during masturbation or oral sex.

During intercourse, the more of this fluid that a man produces the better, because it can make the head of his penis much more slippery and therefore make the penetration of his lover's vagina much more comfortable. Some physicians argue that lubrication isn't the primary purpose of this fluid, and they may be right, since (unaided) it simply oozes out of the opening in the penis rather than smothering the whole glans. But a deft finger massage can cover the glans with it in an instant, and whether the fluid is meant to be a lubricant or not, it certainly *works* like one.

If a man holds off the moment of penetration for as long as possible, he will find that a considerable amount of this fluid has been emitted. He can then guide his lover's hand down to his erect penis, and have her massage the slippery stuff all over the head for him. Apart from being functional, this small act will give her evidence of the fact that she has aroused him, and this, in turn, will arouse her. The wetness that women experience when they are ready for sex is often talked about; but very little mention is made of this pre-ejaculatory fluid that men leak out.

Here's Brad, 22, a trainee computer salesman from Birmingham, Alabama: "Sure I'd been out with girls before, but Cindy was fantastic. She dynamited my mind, she truly did. She had all of this wavy brunette hair and lips like an angel and these long eyelashes that practically blew you away with the draft when she batted them. I took her out for barbecued ribs and then we went for a drive. We parked by the lake and started petting. She kissed like she was still hungry, and she wanted to eat me, and she kept lifting her leg up and rubbing it against my leg. She's something else, I have to tell you. She has this really full bosom and these long, long legs and she was wearing a red checkered blouse and the tightest shortest denim halter-top shorts you ever saw. I unclipped her halter top and I slid my hand inside her blouse. She was wearing only a half-cup bra, and so her nipples were bare. I rolled her nipples around with my fingers and I was in heaven with a capital H. Then I unbuttoned her blouse and bared her breasts. They were big and soft and suntanned brown, so she must have been sunbathing nude. They just nestled in that white lacy half-cup bra, going up and down, up and down, when she breathed. I had a hard-on like an iron bar, and when I started kissing her again, and fondling her breasts, she took hold of my hard-on through my pants, and started rubbing it up and down. In the end she tugged open my zipper, and slipped her hand inside my shorts. She took hold of my bare cock and rubbed it sl-o-o-owly up and down. Then she eased it out of my pants. She slowly squeezed the shaft upwards, gripping it real hard. She squeezed up a drop of clear juice, and when it was trembling right on the top of my cock, she stuck out her tongue and licked it. She did that four or five times, and then she licked her lips and said, 'I love that stuff.' I'd never realized before that I had so much of it."

Most men find that continued sexual stimulation (e.g., watching pornographic videos or reading erotic literature) will encourage the secretion of a certain amount of pre-ejaculatory fluid. And anal stimulation before intercourse can have the same effect, especially if it involves firm massage of the front of the rectal wall, about a thumb's-length inside the anus. In fact a woman can massage a man in this way, and without touching his penis at all, produce an unusually copious amount of fluid, and even bring him to a full climax.

If she does it *during* intercourse, or uses a dildo or an anal stimulator in the same way, she can greatly increase the strength of his climax.

During foreplay and intercourse, a man becomes highly sensitive to any stimulation around the genital area, yet it's surprising how many women, during lovemaking, don't ever fondle their lover's balls or anus, or feel their own vaginal lips with their fingers, so that they can enjoy this physical joining-together with even greater intensity.

Some women express a dislike of touching themselves sexually, "especially when I'm so wet." Others feel that they might be interfering in some way with their lover's performance. In actual fact, most men greatly enjoy the feeling of having their penis touched while they're having intercourse, and they are flattered and aroused by feeling a woman parting her vaginal lips even wider with one or both hands so that they can enter her even more deeply.

The woman herself can benefit greatly from touching herself during intercourse. Some women like to play with their clitorises during intercourse, or even (in certain positions, such as the rear-entry position) masturbate themselves at full speed. This doesn't reflect badly on the man's sexual prowess: it simply means that the woman will become aroused more surely and more quickly, and increase the chances of a simultaneous or near-simultaneous orgasm.

During intercourse, the rate of a man's breathing increases from 12 to 16 breaths per minute to 40 or even 50 breaths a minute. The heart pumps blood more quickly, a condition known as *tachycardia*. The heart rate increases in direct proportion to the level of sexual arousal, so that the heart beats most rapidly at the moment of climax. A man's normal heart rate is 72 beats per minute, but during intercourse a heart rate of 110 to 180 is quite common. His blood pressure increases, too, a condition known as *hypertension*.

This, of course, is why good basic health is essential for peak-performance sex. The healthier a man is, the lower his heart rate, and the less it will rise during sexual excitement. He will have more stamina, he will enjoy his climax more—and will decrease his chances of a heart attack.

I'm not suggesting that peak-performance sex depends on endless hours of jogging and working out. Intensive exercise isn't suitable for everyone. But every man should do his utmost to keep himself in good physical condition—by walking for at least a half-hour each day, until he breaks into a sweat, or by using a rowing machine or an exercise cycle at home or in a gym. Women should do so as well.

If you find this kind of regime boring, try attaching a book rack to the handlebars of your exercise cycle, or wearing a personal stereo when you go for walks, to play any kind of tape you like. If you're really dedicated to peak-performance sex, you can buy audio sex cassettes, with such titles as *Listen to Me Suck* and *Audio Orgy*, and stimulate yourself while you exercise.

One of the very best exercises for sexual stamina is the push-up. If you haven't done push-ups lately, start with just five, and gradually work up to twenty a day. Do them as slowly as possible, for maximum strength and maximum control.

There are plenty of healthy low-cholesterol diets available, which apart from helping to keep a man healthier and fitter, will also improve body shape (all those with beer-guts and love-handles please take note!). Make losing any excess weight part of your peak-performance sex plan (over a reasonable period of time). You'll be gratified by the difference it makes in your lovemaking; and you'll also be gratified by your lover's response to the way you look.

Having a strong sense of your own attractiveness to your lover is an essential part of sexual fulfillment. And—although your lover may think that you're 110 percent perfect—you will never totally believe her if you don't feel self-confident about your appearance, your physique, and your sexual skills.

That's why it's worthwhile to make an effort to lose weight and stay trim. If you *feel* better and *look* better, you'll make love better.

On the subject of diet, I'm frequently asked if there are any known substances that (a) directly increase a man's sexual virility, and (b) act as aphrodisiacs.

As far as virility is concerned, the best known substances are a balanced diet (plenty of fruit, vegetables, fresh fish, lean meat, and whole-grain breads). There are no magic vitamins that improve a man's virility, and even if you do take extra vitamins, in the hope of increasing your stamina, your body will simply excrete all those that are superfluous to its normal daily requirements.

Ginseng root is supposed to keep a man young and sexually active, but it contains nothing that scientifically substantiates this claim. Royal jelly is also touted as a panacea for aging and impotence, but again, there is no rational evidence to indicate that what's good for bees is equally good for humans.

As far as aphrodisiacs are concerned, the answer is simply: there aren't any. You can eat all the oysters in the bay, but they won't have any effect on your sexual desire or the rigidity of your penis. A number of spurious products are sold under the names of Spanish Fly Love Capsules ("will get you ready, hold you steady, and shortly you'll be raring to go"); Muira Puama ("get and give the pleasure a full, firm thrusting penis can deliver"); Love Sugar ("use instead of normal sugar in drinks, it's a powerful aphrodisiac . . . gives startling results"). There's even Powdered Rino Horn—yes, note the spelling of "rino"—"the famous back-to-nature recipe, dissolved in a drink it will arouse the animal in you and your partner"; and (my personal favorite for sheer effrontery) Fire Drops—formulated by a doctor subsequently struck off the medical register, Fire Drops were conceived to "slip" into any drink, having no color, taste or smell . . . 20 drops is sufficient to induce a woozy sensation and to cause primary swelling of the clitoris.

None of these or any similar products have the slightest aphrodisiac effect, and they definitely don't contain any real rhinoceros horn (not that *that* has any aphrodisiac effect, either) or real Spanish fly. The real Spanish fly, incidentally, is made from the crushed cantharis or blister beetle, and is an extremely unpleasant and even dangerous genitourinary irritant. The infamous lover Casanova gave it to a girl in the hope of having an especially good time, but it killed her.

I cannot emphasize strongly enough that *there are no lotions, no creams, no pills, no sprays that will ever have any effect on your virility, your sexual passion, or the rigidity of your penis*. If I knew something that *did* have such an effect, I would have marketed it years ago and retired to the Bahamas a multimillionaire.

Some drugs, such as amyl nitrate, are claimed to have aphrodisiac effects, but the dangers of using drugs to heighten sexual sensation are extreme. Numerous fatalities have occurred from the use of amyl nitrate—mostly from heart attacks—and after continual use the effects of the drug are considerably diminished.

People who rely on drugs to intensify their sexual responses *invariably* lose their ability to have sex freely and spontaneously, and in a comparatively short time they can lose their sexual responses, too. This is not moralistic finger-wagging, this is a clinically observed fact.

Peak-performance sex can be achieved without any artificial aids whatsoever—dietary, mechanical, or chemical.

This is also an appropriate time to mention penis developers. These are clear plastic cylinders out of which the air can be extracted with a hand-operated pump. You insert your penis into the cylinder through a plastic seal (to prevent any air leaking back into the cylinder) and pump out the air. Anybody who studied high-school physics knows that nature abhors a vacuum, so your penis will swell to an enormous size to compensate for the missing air. Some of the developers have multispeed vibrators attached so that you can masturbate while you develop—"staying continuously erect and exploding into a vacuum."

I have nothing against these so-called developers as sex toys or aids to masturbation. It's quite amusing to see your flaccid penis steadily grow as you pump out the air. If a man has been suffering repeated failures in achieving or sustaining an erection, a penis developer might be helpful in restoring his confidence in his ability to get hard again, and I can think of no better reason for buying one than that. But I must caution you that if you're thinking of buying one in order to enlarge your penis, save your money. Penis developers *don't* permanently increase the size of your member—or, if they do, they increase it so infinitesimally that the increase can scarcely be measured.

11

The Double-Quick Erection

As you work your way toward peak performance, it's useful to train your mind and your body to work in close conjunction with each other to achieve the fastest erection possible. The reason for this training is to give both confidence in your ability to rise on demand and superior control over your penis once it *has* risen.

Normally, of course, your penis will rise involuntarily when you start to make love, but what happens if it doesn't? And what happens if it subsides during foreplay, or halfway through intercourse? What do you do then?

One thing you *never* do is panic, or lose confidence in your ability to regain an erection. You can control your erections much more than you might imagine—through both mental and physical self-conditioning—and also by educating your lover to give you encouragement and assistance when the going gets soft.

You will need a notepad for the following training. Over a two-week period—if you follow the exercises religiously—you should not only be able to achieve a fully hard erection whenever you want to, but you should be able to achieve it in less than half the time that it takes you now.

Divide your notepad into 14 squares, one for each day of your training. Then divide each square into sections for Time to Erection, Time to Climax, Time to Resolution, Length, Girth, and Remarks. The only other equipment you'll need for this exercise is a tape measure, a stopwatch if you have one, or a watch with a sweep second hand; and a pen.

Each day *at the same time* find a room where you can be alone without fear of interruption. I realize that this isn't always easy, but do try. The room should preferably be warm and comfortable, but if you're forced by circumstances to use a bathroom or restroom, then that will have to do. Obviously you won't be nearly so relaxed in a restroom, and your results may not be as dramatic as they would have been had you been able to carry out the exercise in the privacy of your own bedroom, but they should still show *comparative* improvement.

If you're able to, remove all of your clothes and adopt a position which *you* find most comfortable for masturbation. You should have no erotic photographs or sexy magazines nearby—no artificial stimulants. All of the stimulation should come from within your own mind, which is one of the ways in which you will train both your mind and your penis to work in close coordination.

Start your stopwatch, and at the same time commence masturbating as fast as you possibly can. The aim is to climax *quickly*. While you're masturbating, think of all the most arousing things you can. They could be tried-and-trusted sexual fantasies that always turn you on. They could be ways in which you'd like to make love to your wife or girlfriend. Or they could simply be the feelings you're getting from standing naked in a room in the middle of the day, furiously masturbating yourself.

If you didn't have an erection to begin with, make a quick note of how long it takes you to reach full hardness. Then masturbate as fast and as hard as you can toward a climax, concentrating only on whatever excites you the most.

Learn to be narrow-minded. Learn to think about nothing else except your heightened state of sexual excitement, and the fantasies that are bringing you closer and closer to climax. Your whole being is inside your penis, bursting to be released.

This is Kevin, 28, a department-store salesman from White Plains, New York: "I have this recurring fantasy that I've been kidnapped by about fifteen girls from a girls' school. They drag me into their dormitory and undress me; and then *they* undress, too. They touch me and fondle me and suck my cock, one after the other. They push their tits into my face and rub their tits all over my body. There's nothing I can do. I'm pinned down to the bed and there's too many of them. They start to jerk me off, rubbing me real quick. That's when my fantasy starts to kind of coincide with reality. I'm fantasizing that the hand that's rubbing my cock is one of the girls' hands, not mine. I use really light, quick strokes, just touching my glans with my fingertips. Sometimes I'm stroking my balls with my other hand; and I make out that *this* is being done by another girl. I imagine that one of the girls sits on my face, pushing her cunt right up against my mouth so that I can hardly breathe, squashing it around and around so that my face is covered in cunt-juice. She's leaning over my cock with her mouth open, waiting for the come to fly. That's usually about as far as I ever have to fantasize, because then I shoot my load."

Many more men reported using similar fantasies while they masturbated—although almost all of them said that they used fantasies in a very different way when they made love to their wives or girl-friends, and considerably less often. "I *do* sometimes fantasize when I'm making love to Freda, but she becomes an integral part of the fantasy," said Leonard, 35, from San Francisco. "She's usually a slave girl, although she doesn't know it. I've bought her in the market or else she's been given to me. She has to be naked all the time, and I'm entitled to fuck her whenever I want to, as often as I want to."

I was interested in knowing what Freda would have thought of this fantasy. "I'm not sure. It happens inside my own head. I've never told her about it. Sometimes it's just a feeling and it's gone in a flash. I think she'd think that I was weird."

I persuaded Leonard to tell Freda about it, and far from thinking that he was "weird" she found the fantasy flattering and exciting. After that, they acted it out several times together, even to the extent of tying Freda's wrists and ankles to the bed with scarves, and covering her mouth with a scarf. Both of them said that this game had renewed their interest in sex, and Leonard remarked, "It took my fantasy out of my head and into the bedroom, for real."

The instant you climax—when the first spurt of semen shoots out—press your stopwatch button and record exactly how long it took you to reach orgasm from a "standing start." You can also make a note of roughly how much semen you ejaculated, and how many spasms you experienced.

The first time you masturbate like this, you'll probably climax quite quickly. But on the second and third and fourth days, when you return to your room at the same time to masturbate once again, you'll find it takes you a great deal longer to stiffen and to reach a climax. You'll also find that your attention begins to wander, since—physiologically, at any rate—you've been having quite enough sex this week to keep you satisfied.

This is the moment when your concentration and

your training really come into play. You may not
feel like climaxing, you may not even feel like masturbating. But rouse the strongest images you can
from your imagination, and at the same time rub
your penis in the most stimulating way, as fast and
as hard as you can. Keep flexing the perineal muscle
between your legs as you masturbate. This will help
you to keep your erection and will encourage the
production of seminal fluid in your prostate gland.

It doesn't matter how extreme your fantasies may
be. The aim is to achieve the fastest erection in the
West—followed by the fastest climax. By the fifth or
sixth day you should be seeing some signs that your
concentration is improving, and by the tenth day
you should be able to feel a heightened degree of
control over the erection of your penis and over the
timing of your climax.

You will probably notice that you are not ejaculating as much semen as you did on the very first day,
but the copiousness of your ejaculation will increase
as your control over your perineal muscle increases—
mainly because you are stimulating your prostate to
produce more seminal fluid.

Not every day will see an improvement. But you
will learn by your setbacks. You will learn which
fantasies are guaranteed to fire your erection and
which aren't. You will probably create new fantasies, even more erotic than before. You will also
learn how to increase your concentration.

Peak-performance sex depends on your being
wholly engrossed in what you are doing—wholly
engrossed in giving pleasure to your partner; wholly
engrossed in enjoying the pleasure that your partner
gives you in return.

Many people who have learned to meditate have
found that their ability to clear their mind of petty
anxieties and irrelevant external pressures is quite

helpful in preparing themselves for lovemaking. As 27-year-old Denise, from Los Angeles, told me: "You can't enjoy making love to the full when half of your mind is still trying to deal with the household budget or what you're going to cook for supper tomorrow. There used to be a time when I had only half of my mind on making love. It was only when Rick said to me, 'What the hell's the matter with you, you're so *frigid*?' that I realized what I was doing. Sex was becoming routine, like shopping. I was making love the same way I walked around Ralph's market, or collected the children from school."

After two weeks of high-speed masturbation, you should find that your ability to attain an erection quickly and your ability to ejaculate more promptly have noticeably improved. You can carry out this high-speed masturbation exercise at any time—not necessarily for the entire two weeks, but for as long as it takes to refocus your concentration and tone up your sexual responsiveness.

Interestingly, high-speed masturbation exercises can also help men who suffer from premature ejaculation. Although it would seem that the very *last* thing that these men need is an ability to reach a climax quickly, the ejaculatory control that these exercises provide works equally well for *any* problem that a man may have in achieving an erection and reaching a desired climax.

If, after two weeks of high-speed masturbation exercises, a man is *still* suffering from premature ejaculation difficulties, he can then switch to very slow masturbation exercises. These involve masturbating firmly but slowly, and *pausing* whenever a climax seems to be imminent. In other words, he should delay the moment of ejaculatory inevitability for as long as possible, while continuing to stimulate himself sexually.

After three weeks of slow masturbation exercises, a man who "almost always" ejaculated as soon as he entered his partner's vagina found that he was able to keep up intercourse without ejaculation for "three or four minutes at first . . . until I started to get anxious about it"—but then for "five minutes, and more, and then as long as I wanted." Unconsciously, he had begun to understand that his penis was not a separate entity over which he had no control, but was a controllable part of his own being.

A man needn't necessarily carry out high- (or low-) speed masturbation exercises on his own. Depending on his personal circumstances, and the nature of his sexual situation, it can be very helpful if the woman in his life assists him in reaching a climax.

Clyde, a 32-year-old oil-rigger from Pascagoula, Mississippi, said: "I always had a problem from coming too soon. It started with my first wife, who was two years older than me. It always seemed like *she* was in charge of our relationship, and I guess that made me nervous . . . gave me a hair-trigger ejaculation. Sometimes I'd only have to touch her pussy and I shot out all over the damn place. When I got married the second time (to Belinda) I was okay at first, but then I started to get anxious about my sexual performance again, and the same thing started to happen . . . the hair-trigger climax. I tried the high-speed masturbation. I didn't see how it could help me, since my problem was coming too quick and I didn't think I needed to know how to come any quicker. But in fact it did give me more control over my ejaculation, because it gave me more control over my total self. I began to feel that I was in charge of my body and how it responded."

After two weeks of high-speed masturbation on his own, Clyde tried a week of very low-speed masturbation with Belinda. The object of this was for Clyde to delay his climax for as long as he possibly could, while at the same time giving Belinda experience in gripping his penis in a way that would delay his ejaculation time and time again.

"We lay naked side by side on the bed, and Belinda very slowly massaged my cock until it was hard. I felt like I wanted her to do it more quickly, but she did it real slow, up and down, up and down, squeezing the shaft and massaging the glans with her fingertips.

"I began to feel the first twitches of a climax after only a few moments—deep down between my legs. The juice started to flow out of my cock, and soon Belinda was massaging the glans with a whole lot of slippery lubricant. I knew that it would only take two or three more strokes for me to come, so I told her to stop, and she gripped my cock real tight, with her thumb pressing just below the opening in the glans; and twisted my cock around a little, with a turn of her wrist; and gradually the feeling died down.

"We did this again and again, and my hard-on lasted for nearly forty-five minutes. I'd never kept it up for so long without climaxing . . . even though by this time I was just about aching to come. Each time I felt that I was on the brink, I told Belinda to stop, and she'd stop massaging and grip me that same way.

"At last we decided that I'd managed to hold off climaxing for long enough. Belinda climbed on top of me and guided my cock up into her pussy. I used not to like her sitting on top of me . . . it used to give me the feeling that I wasn't in control, that I wasn't really a man. But now I felt different about it. I pushed my cock deep up inside her. I raised my hips so that I practically lifted her off the bed, and my cock went up so far that it touched her womb and made her shout out.

"I kept on thrusting and thrusting and I suddenly realized that I wasn't about to shoot out directly—I could control my own sensitivity and my own climax. Belinda climaxed first, which was amazing—the first time she'd ever done it before me. I could feel her pussy rippling and clutching my cock like you wouldn't believe. It was then that I came, too, and it was amazing. I pumped about five or six times; and I thought that I was going to black out. Just amazing. Belinda lifted herself off me, and sperm literally poured out of her open pussy and down her thigh."

Clyde was a classic case of a man suffering from premature ejaculation. His marital relationship with his first wife was largely responsible for his condition continuing. As Masters and Johnson remarked in *Human Sexual Inadequacy*: "An impotent man views his wife as especially threatening to his self-confidence. She is the one person who knows the full extent of his failure: he may feel that he cannot be a man in her presence. A sexually frustrated woman will sometimes obtain revenge or justification of her shrewishness by spreading word of her husband's inadequacy or belittling him in other ways. If this situation exists, the wife in treatment must be urged emphatically to cooperate."

Clyde's first wife—although he spoke about her in a very gentlemanly way—regarded his premature ejaculation as a personal slight, as if he wasn't really interested in satisfying her at all. Her attitude was quite understandable, because sexual frustration can distort anybody's view of even the most loving relationship. But she was not prepared to help him correct it, and when he suggested seeking professional counseling, she refused to participate, telling him that "all you have to do is act like a man."

A man's inability to achieve erection or to control his climax rarely reflects how he feels about his lover. Most of the men with whom I have spoken about premature ejaculation were passionately in love with their partners, and highly sexually aroused by them. Only problem: they had lost confidence in their ability to satisfy them, and for one reason or another found it almost impossible to regain that confidence.

"Sometimes I'd manage to get an erection, and then I'd suddenly think, 'I've made it, I've got an erection! I hope to God it lasts.' And because I'd thought about it, because I'd worried about it, it sank straight down again. I could have wept, believe me. I could have wept."

The grip that Belinda used on Clyde in order to delay his orgasm was a modified version of the "squeeze technique," which was discovered by Masters and Johnson during their sex-therapy sessions with men who suffered from premature ejaculation. It was astonishingly successful—during an eleven-year period 186 men were treated for premature ejaculation at the Masters and Johnson Foundation in St. Louis, Missouri, and only 4 failed to respond.

As the man approaches a climax, his partner grips his penis tightly, with her index finger curled around the shaft just below the ridge of his glans, with the ball of her thumb pressed hard against the frenum (the thin membrane of skin just below the opening in his glans).

Usually, a 5- to 10-second squeeze is sufficient to hold back a man's climax. The purpose, of course, is to show him that he *can* keep an erection for a considerable length of time.

The couples who tried out this technique for the

purposes of Peak-Performance Sex found that the squeeze was even more effective if it was accompanied by a twisting-around of the man's erect penis, up to a 90-degree turn, so that the opening in the glans was actually facing sideways. Wives and lovers should be reassured that a man's erect penis can be squeezed very hard indeed without any discomfort or injury.

Eventually the moment comes when a man *wants* to climax. In fact, once he passes the stage of ejaculatory inevitability, he's going to climax whether he wants to or not.

The outward signs of an approaching male climax are that a man starts to thrust more quickly into his partner's vagina, clutching her tightly, and—in the split-second before ejaculation—pushes himself into her as hard and as deep as he can.

From the moment that a male climax is inevitable, all of a man's secondary sexual organs are involved in expelling seminal fluid into the prostatic urethra. At this time—the first stage in male orgasm—all of the muscles in a man's pelvis contract involuntarily, very like the way in which a woman's pelvic muscles go into spasm during *her* climax.

Sperm cells flow from the testes through emptying ducts called the *vasa efferentia*, up into the man's body through the *epididymis*, which is that curly tubing that you can feel when you touch a man's testicles. From there, the sperm cells travel through another tube called the *vas deferens* until they reach a little storage sac, known as the *ampulla*. Here they wait until the moment of ejaculation.

At the same time that the sperm cells have been making their way to the *ampulla*, the prostate gland is rhythmically contracting and squeezing out the whitish mucus that forms the basis of semen. Additional fluid is added from the *seminal vesicle*.

When the *seminal vesicle* discharges its fluid, the sperm cells are ejected from the *ampulla* to mix with the seminal fluid in the prostatic urethra. At the same time, the urethral bulb behind the scrotum is enlarged in volume, in preparation for the final forcible ejaculation.

Within a split second before ejaculation, the internal muscle of the bladder tightens up, preventing semen from being forced into the bladder, and also ensuring that the ejaculation has only one way to go—and under the greatest pressure possible. The tightening of this muscle also ensures that no urine can escape during ejaculation.

Next, the external muscle of the bladder relaxes, in opposition to all of the other muscles in the pelvis. Scientists still don't understand how this nervous reflex works, but it allows the seminal fluid to flow from the prostate urethra to the enlarged bulb at the base of the penis. You could compare this bulb with the rubber bulb of an old-fashioned motor horn.

When the bulb is filled with fluid, it contracts, so that seminal fluid is ejected out of the penis. At the same time, two large muscles in the floor of the man's pelvis also go into spasm, adding to the force of the climax.

If there were nothing in the way, a man's ejaculation would travel up to 2 feet away—occasionally farther.

The contractions of the man's secondary sex organs occur three or four times, slightly more than once a second.

Climax to the Max

A man can add to the force of his climax in several ways. One way is by holding it back for as long as he possibly can. This not only adds to *his* pleasure, it adds to his lover's pleasure, too. But holding back a climax isn't as easy as it sounds. A man's natural instinct is to ejaculate as quickly as possible, thus ensuring, of course, that his mate is impregnated as quickly as possible. Back in the dawn of time, when the survival of the species was critical, men didn't concern themselves with improving the quality of their climax, and it wasn't important whether women had orgasms.

There are several ways in which a man can delay his climax. Which one *you* prefer depends on your sexual sensitivity. If you tend to ejaculate too quickly, then you will probably consider removing your penis from your lover's vagina completely, and even applying the squeeze-and-twist technique. You can do this as many times as you want to—and up to a point you will find that your subsequent climax is increasingly explosive. You can, however, do it a little too often, and pass the peak of your sexual excitement. You will be able to discover the number of times for withdrawal and squeezing that works best for *you* only by repeated practice. Obviously it is more desirable for your lover to do the squeezing, but you can do it just as effectively yourself.

You may find that you prefer simply to withdraw your penis during intercourse and continue to stimulate your lover in other ways. This has the effect of delaying your climax but maintaining *her* gradually increasing momentum toward an orgasm.

This technique found favor from 33-year-old Sherri, a sales assistant from Austin, Texas, when it was tried by her 31-year-old husband, Rick, a real-estate salesman. "Rick never quite managed to last long enough. I don't know whether it was his fault because he always came too quickly, or my fault because I always came too slowly. Or maybe it wasn't anybody's actual *fault*. But all the same I was always left frustrated, even if he finished me off with his tongue or his fingers . . . and Rick was always left with the feeling that he hadn't managed to satisfy me properly.

"So we tried taking his cock out of me halfway through making love. It isn't as easy as it sounds. I mean foreplay naturally leads to intercourse and then intercourse naturally leads to having a climax. It seems kind of unnatural to take it out right in the middle, but we did it.

"The first time, we were making love in a motel in Corpus Christi, where we'd gone to spend the weekend with friends. I don't know whether it helped, being away from home in a different place, but we did feel a bit more like lovers than man and wife, if you understand what I mean.

"Rick wined me and dined me with a good steak and a bottle of red wine. We took another bottle back to our room. As soon as he had closed the door, he started kissing me and caressing me like he really wanted me; and it's good to get *that* from your husband, too—especially when you're a couple of years older, like I am, and you always need that 10 percent more reassurance that you're still just as sexually attractive to him as you've always been.

"He slid down the zipper of my dress, and let it drop to the floor. He kissed me some more, and stroked my back, and touched my breasts through my bra, gently rubbing his thumb against my nipples so that they stood up under the satin. I wasn't wearing panties, only pantyhose, and he cupped his hand between my legs and stroked me with his finger. I could feel that my pantyhose were wet. In fact, they had been for most of the evening, because the atmosphere was so romantic and I just knew that we were going to make love.

"Rick unfastened my bra and took it off. He squeezed and caressed my breasts and kissed and sucked at my nipples. I've always thought that my breasts were far too big. Once I even went to my doctor to talk about a reduction. But Rick loves them . . . he loves to caress them and bury his face in them, so what can I do? He's my husband and he's my lover, and the way he wants me is the way I am.

"He led me over to the bed and lay me down, and carried on kissing and caressing me. He really knows how to kiss. Some guys kiss like they think it's something they're supposed to do, but all they want to do is get it over with so that they can get on with the fucking. Rick never kisses like that. He kisses like he's sharing his soul. It really helps to get me excited, the way he kisses like that; and it shows that he loves me and he cares about me, and I think that's one of the really important things about sex. I've known so many guys who treat it like something mechanical; like they're repairing their car or something.

"He rolled off my pantyhose, and while he was doing that I unbuttoned his shirt and unbuckled his belt. He's quite skinny and muscular, and I love to run my hands over his back and his bare chest. His cock was rearing up inside his shorts, and I slipped my hand inside and rubbed it and caressed it. It felt hot and very hard and so-o-o good. I wriggled down underneath him and pulled off his pants, and then I took his cock in my mouth and gave it a good sucking and licking. There's nothing like the taste of a man's cock when you just pull it out of his shorts . . . it's not like he's taken a shower or anything. He tastes of turned-on man, not Badedas, if you know what I mean.

"Rick stroked my thighs and caressed me between my legs. He has a way of gently rolling my clitoris around between his finger and thumb, gently, gently, so that after a while I begin to feel this beautiful warm urge between my legs. I reached down and helped him to slide his cock into my pussy, and then he started slowly to fuck me—very, very slowly. I lifted my head and looked down, and I could see his cock sliding in and out of me, burying itself right inside me, so that our pubic hair was all entangled together and I didn't know whose pubic hair was which.

"We already knew that we were going to try holding off his climax by taking out his cock, but I can tell you for a fact that right then I didn't want to. I just wanted him to go on fucking me it felt so good. It seemed to fill me right up, it was so big and hot and slippery, and I could feel his balls jogging against the cheeks of my bottom with every stroke.

"But I could feel him beginning to speed up after just two or three minutes, and I knew that he was getting turned on too quickly. That's what *always* happened, and that was the problem. So I took hold of his cock and slipped it out of my pussy, and I said to him, 'Come on, Rick, let's try this technique . . . it really could work.'

"He climbed over and knelt beside me on the bed, and kissed me some more, and kissed my breasts. I held up my breast in my hand and pushed my nipple into his mouth, so that he had a big mouthful. He likes to gently suck my nipples and flick them with the tip of his tongue at the same time . . . and I like it, too.

"At the same time, he carried on flicking my clitoris with his fingertip, so that he was still turning me on. The idea is that the woman doesn't go off the boil . . . and it was good, it worked. You get a different kind of arousal from having your clitoris rubbed than you do when you're actually being fucked, but it's just as exciting . . . it's just as much of a turn-on, and I liked the idea that while he was kissing me and fingering me he was slowing himself down while I was catching up with him.

"He knelt close beside me and I turned my face to the side and took his cock into my mouth. This time it tasted of *me*, as well as him. I sucked it very gently, taking care not to turn him on too much, and I squeezed the shaft tight, the way I was told, to hold back his climax.

"He Was Rock-Hard and He Was Slow"

"When his cock was all slippery with my saliva, he massaged my breasts with it, circling the head around my nipples. I pushed my breasts together and he slowly fucked my cleavage. I could see the dark red head of his cock appearing and reappearing between my breasts; and my cleavage was all warm and shiny with his juice.

"Then he climbed back on top of me and pushed his cock back inside my pussy. I can't tell you . . . I really needed it by then. The feeling was tremendous. He was rock-hard and he was slow, and he was giving me everything he had.

"I don't know how I managed to reach an orgasm. It kind of took me by surprise. One second he was slowly fucking me, the next I was jumping and squealing like a cat on a hot tin roof. I was still in the middle of muscle spasms when Rick gave me five or six quick hard strokes with his cock and then he climaxed, too. He said something but I don't know what it was, and he can't remember either.

"I'd never felt his sperm come out of him before, but I did then. It was like I could feel the head of his cock *bulge*, almost, and then all this warmth flooding inside me. I had some more spasms. In fact I must have had six or seven or maybe more, and when it was all over I felt like a *dishrag*, completely fucked out.

"There was kind of an aftermath. I sat on the toilet afterward and Rick came in. I said, 'Look, this is all yours,' and opened up my legs so that he could see his sperm dripping out of me. He stood close to me and kissed my hair, and I held his half-stiff cock and opened my lips and took all of it into my mouth. There was still some sperm in the shaft of his cock and I sucked it out of him like milkshake out of a straw. He started to get hard again, and the next thing I knew we were back on the bed, doing it again. Rick didn't come that time, but I did, after only a couple of minutes. It was a delicious twitchy sensation, really fantastic. For the first time I began to realize how much sex we had in us, Rick and me . . . and just how good it could be."

Obviously, different men will respond differently. Some men would have found that—if their lovers gave them oral sex halfway through intercourse— they would have climaxed more quickly instead of more slowly. Again, it's a question of practice and self-exploration. I have talked with several men who are so breast-oriented that they only have to touch their penises against their lovers' nipples and they ejaculate almost immediately.

The perineal muscle, which is located in the floor

of the pelvis, is one of the muscles that spasm during a man's climax; this spasm not only propels his semen further, but intensifies the erotic sensation he feels at the moment of ejaculation. If you flex this muscle a few times right now—right where you're sitting—you should experience a mildly pleasurable feeling between your legs.

Flex this muscle whenever possible and for as long as possible. When you're working at your desk, when you're flying on a business trip, when you're driving your car. Then, when you come to the moment of climax, *consciously* flex it as hard as you can. This isn't easy, but once you learn to get the timing right, you will find that you can improve the enjoyment of your climax.

"It took me four or five times to get it right. But one morning my wife and I were making love and I consciously squeezed that muscle between my legs and, boy, I felt like I was rocket-propelled. It went into spasm and it kept on and on, and I had the best damn climax in the history of climaxes."

12

Specialized Stimulation . . . and Then Some

Another dramatic way in which a man's climax can be intensified is by anal stimulation during intercourse. There are several ways in which this can be done, and how *you* do it will depend on your personal tastes and responses. Some couples are reluctant to include anal stimulation in their lovemaking because they're afraid that it might prove to be dirty, but there is rarely any fecal matter in the rectum, and if you take care to wash your hands and any sex aids thoroughly after anal stimulation, you should encounter no problems or unpleasantness whatsoever.

Some sex-aid catalogs advertise "cinnamon-flavored intimate sexual lubricant" for use with anal sex stimulators "to maximize painless penetration, to alleviate anal discomfort . . . fragranced for total hygiene and to negate any unpleasant odors." You don't need to go as far as buying any of *that*, but anal stimulation is usually made more comfortable with some kind of lubricant, such as KY.

As we have seen, it is possible for a woman to insert her finger into her lover's anus and by forcefully massaging the front wall of his rectum, to stimulate his prostate gland. This will eventually give him a feeling of deep sexual pleasure, and intensify his climax. It can even increase the volume of his ejaculation.

The drawbacks to this method of anal stimulation are that not all men enjoy it—especially during the first few minutes, when the sensation of having their prostate massaged can be more of a turn-off than a turn-on. "A very weird sensation," said one man. "I don't know whether I liked it or not." There is also the problem that most women have long fingernails, which at the very least makes anal probing uncomfortable, and at the very worst, injurious.

However, both men and women can obtain some safe and sensational anal stimulation from the various sex aids on the market. There is an "anal vibro kit," which includes a narrow-diameter multispeed vibrator, on to which you can fit three different latex sleeves for varying sensations. One is covered in small knobbly protrusions; another is shaped like a very slim male penis, complete with glans and veiny shaft; a third is long and fingerlike, with a wide knobble-covered base.

The most ancient of all anal stimulators—love beads—are still being marketed in modern versions. Chinese love beads are a string of five small plastic beads, which are lightly lubricated and then squeezed into the anus one by one before intercourse. There is a brass ring on the end of the string that should be slowly tugged as a man ejaculates, so that the beads ripple out of his anus and intensify his climax.

Thai love beads are similar but smaller, and attached to a stiffer plastic thread, with a handle at the base so that they can be oscillated inside the rectum during intercourse—and then tugged out at the moment of climax.

Any vibrator can be used for anal stimulation, but you should obviously avoid using any object that could be lost inside the rectum. This could be painful, and could even necessitate a surgical operation to remove it. Like all other sexual acts, anal stimulation calls for common sense.

Probably the best anal stimulator on the market is the vibrating butt plug, a spigot-shaped vibrator of soft plastisol, with a very wide base to prevent it from being pushed too far inside the rectum. It comes complete with a "raging multispeed vibrating mechanism," and the reports I have received from couples who have used it during intercourse have been nothing short of ecstatic. Many couples like to buy two, so that they can *both* be anally vibrated as they make love.

It Has "Super-Squirmy Double-action"

Another device for giving anal stimulation to both man and woman during lovemaking is the extra-long double-ended dildo, popularly sold as "Doctor David's Double Dong." It has "super-squirmy double-action," and can be inserted into both of your anuses at once, or into *her* vagina and *his* anus, while he penetrates her anus with his penis.

Some men who have had difficulty in sustaining a full erection throughout intercourse—and who subsequently have had trouble in reaching a climax—have discovered that anal intercourse with their lovers can have an extremely therapeutic effect. Because it is so much tighter than her vagina, a woman's anus gives strong and continuous massage during intercourse, and she can also flex her anal sphincter very powerfully to intensify her grip on her lover's penis.

John, a 29-year-old construction engineer from Boise, Idaho, went through "seven months of misery and frustration" before a regimen of anal sex with his 26-year-old wife Pat restored his confidence in his ability to keep a full erection and to achieve a climax.

"I'd been through a very difficult period at work. We had a couple of bad winters, then a whole lot of layoffs; then one of our clients went bankrupt halfway through a major project, and we almost went to the wall ourselves. Work was always on my mind, and I guess that was why our sex life started to suffer. I'd get aroused okay, and start to make love okay, but then my attention would start to wander, and my cock would soften just a little. Not completely, but enough to reduce the feeling that I got from sliding it in and out of Pat's vagina.

"The net result was that I could never reach a climax, because my cock wasn't being stimulated enough; and of course Pat could never reach a climax, either, because she could sense my frustration, and she could also feel that my cock wasn't totally hard. That made her feel that she didn't really turn me on any longer—that it was all *her* fault. I'm amazed that our marriage managed to survive. I guess the only thing that kept us together was the fact that we loved each other, and because of that, we clung to the belief that, somehow, everything would turn out right.

"But even when business began to get better, my erections stayed under par. I began to think about sex therapy . . . you know, maybe a surrogate lover to get me going again. I even thought about going to a hooker. I didn't want to blame myself so I started to blame Pat, and we had some seriously bad rows.

"I personally wouldn't have considered anal intercourse as a therapy. I'd only done it once before, and not with Pat. I thought that Pat would probably nix the idea, because she's never gone much on my touching her ass, and the few times I've slipped my finger up her anus, she's wriggled her bottom and squeezed me back out again. But after we'd talked about it, she said that she'd give it a try, provided it didn't hurt her. I guess that she was just about as desperate as me. The trouble with sexual problems, they're hard to talk about, even with your wife— maybe *especially* with your wife—because there's always this feeling that you're blaming each other, that a sexual problem has to be somebody's fault. There's always this idea that 'you don't love me as much as I love you.' And you kind of put a shield up, maybe to protect yourself from getting hurt.

"Anyway, we took a tube of KY to bed with us, and we watched a porno video on the bedroom TV to get ourselves into the mood. There was a scene with this secretary-type girl in eyeglasses, she was sitting on the edge of her desk with her skirt lifted, and she was rubbing her pussy and moaning and groaning. Then she took hold of this huge black dildo and started to work it up her asshole. It must have been all of three inches thick, this dildo. I don't know how she got it up there. She had her legs spread so wide apart I thought she was going to crack, but she kept on working this giant thing up her ass, and at the same time rubbing her clitoris and pulling the lips of her cunt.

"While we were watching, I squeezed a little KY on my fingertips, and began to work it around and around Pat's anus. I could feel her pushing against my fingertips, the way she'd been told to. That helped her anus to open up, and I could slip my finger up inside it. It was hot and it was tight. But I kept massaging that KY around it, and in the end I was able to slip a second finger up her. Her muscles flinched a couple of times, practically nipping off my fingers, but she soon remembered to keep pushing against me, so that her anus opened as wide as possible.

"I smoothed some of the KY onto my cock. I was fully hard, totally hard—but then I usually was, when we first started to make love. I stretched her anus as wide as I could with my fingers, then I pushed the head of my cock into it.

"Again she flinched, and her asshole clenched tight. I had to wait for a while, so that she could relax. But on the screen the secretary was on all fours on the rug now, shoving that giant black dildo into herself, and screaming with pleasure, and I guess that made it a little easier for Pat to accept. Eventually I gave two or three firm pushes, and the head of my cock disappeared into her ass, then half of the shaft. At first it felt incredibly tight. It felt so tight that I didn't think I was going to be able to move in and out, to stimulate myself. Her anus clung around the shaft of my cock like a bright red elastic band.

"But then I gently started to ease myself backward and forward, and Pat began to respond. Her anus opened more responsively, and soon I was able to push my cock right inside her. I slid it slowly in and out, and each time I did it I could feel her muscles massaging my shaft, and her anus clinging tight like a suction cup.

"It felt nothing like her cunt. It felt like very hard, deliberate masturbation. I forgot all about losing my erection. My cock seemed to get bigger and harder with every stroke, until I was ramming it in and out of her asshole like a big red piston. It only took her three or four minutes, and she climaxed, forcing her ass hard down into my lap, and making me climax, too. I shot the whole lot deep inside her.

"Afterwards, I thought I might have hurt her. You need to be forceful, to get your cock up there, and to fuck hard enough to reach a climax . . . especially if your woman's a virgin in the ass department. Her asshole was very red and swollen, and the opening looked bigger. But she didn't seem to mind at all. She said she'd enjoyed it; and that she'd do it again anytime I felt like it. To be serious, I think her greatest pleasure came from the fact that after seven months she'd made me come, and that she'd come, too. I went to the bathroom and when I came back she was lying on the bed with her legs apart, watching that sticky white come oozing out of her asshole, as if it was some kind of miracle. I guess in a funny sort of way it was. Anything that could save a sex life that had gotten as messed up as ours just had to be some kind of miracle."

Any additional sensation can add to the pleasure of a man's climax. Some men like a woman to scratch or claw their backs as they ejaculate. Other men enjoy the feeling of crushed ice or mentholated ointment suddenly thrust between their legs. I have come across an extraordinary variety of climax-enhancing stimuli, from chafing a man's buttocks with stiff-bristled hairbrushes to tugging his pubic hair to biting his neck. One 41-year-old husband loved having warm olive oil poured over his back whenever he climaxed. Another liked having a heated hair-roller pushed into his anus (a practice, incidentally, which could have resulted in loss of the hair-roller—far safer to use one of the heat-up vibrators that are now available from sex-aid catalogs, which can be switched on to "hot throbbing erect penis temperature).

When reaching for peak-performance sex, however, never forget that your state of mind is far more important than any device or technique. If you concentrate on giving pleasure—to the exclusion of any other consideration—you will come very close to being the ultimate lover.

You can certainly expect many, many nights that neither of you will ever forget.

We've taken a pretty comprehensive look at ways of heightening a man's sexual enjoyment. Now let's examine . . .

13

Peak Sex for Her

Nowadays, almost all women are aware not only of their *need* to have satisfying sex, but their *right* to expect it, too. In fact, they're entitled to the very peak of sexual pleasure. But with rights come responsibilities, and many women still fail to understand that peak-performance sex depends as much on them as it does on their lovers.

If a woman has an inhibited attitude toward sex, *for whatever reason*, that inhibition can be as serious an obstacle to satisfying lovemaking as a man's inability to achieve an erection.

Before a woman can even think about peak-performance sex, she has to consider the way she feels about her husband and/or lover—not just physically, not just emotionally, but *socially* as well. Sounds odd? Maybe it does. But a woman's sexual response to the man in her life can be seriously impaired not just by anxiety or such ongoing sexual difficulties as premature ejaculation or impotence, but by the way she perceives him as a man.

As Masters and Johnson put it: "A woman's attitudes toward her partner's masculinity, his intelligence, his character traits, his appearance, his drive, any number of variables, have to fit with the requirements of a woman's psychosocial value system for her to respond sexually."

They quoted in particular a couple who had been married for twenty-three years when they were referred for treatment at the Masters and Johnson Foundation. The wife had been able to achieve orgasm and occasionally multiple orgasms during the first twelve years of their marriage. But in the twelfth year, the husband was fired from the company for which he had worked since their wedding. For a year-and-a-half he was unable to find a permanent position. He became depressed and started to drink excessively, and as a result the frequency of their sexual activity decreased.

After a while, the husband started to have an affair, and when the wife found out, there were "vituperative arguments." The wife insisted that they sleep in separate bedrooms.

For about six months the couple had no sexual contact, but during that time the husband found a permanent job, gave up drinking, and stopped seeing the other woman. After a six-month sexual separation, however, the wife found that she was no longer sexually responsive to her husband and that she could not achieve orgasm. She had stopped regarding him as a man, and had lost respect for him and confidence in him. His inability to find a decent job, his drinking, and his affair had changed her feelings about him. As Masters and Johnson put it, "Her psychosocial value system sent enough negative signals to stop her from responding to him sexually."

If a woman harbors any negative feelings about her lover, it is extremely important that she try to identify and reverse them—or at least negate them. At their Foundation, Masters and Johnson used therapists to help women identify the cause of their sexual inhibitions, and to overcome them. You can do the same by making a list of all the things that irritate you about your mate—an honest list—and then asking yourself (a) whether they are really as important to you as you think they are; and (b) if they *are* important, how can you correct them?

"I adored my boyfriend," said 22-year-old Ellen, a publisher's assistant from New York City. "The only trouble was, he always behaved like such a nerd when we went to parties. He would start boasting that he was a world-class chess player and all kinds of insane stuff like that, trying to impress people, and you could tell by the way they edged away from him that they knew he was lying. He was good-looking, he was sexy, he was fun when we were on our own . . . although he kept on trying to lie to me, too. Our lovemaking was terrific to start with, but then I just lost interest. I didn't know who I was supposed to be going to bed with—a world chess champion or an Olympic skier or a thriller-writer ('you won't have heard of my book . . . it was going to be published but the CIA said that the plot was too close to the truth, and they ordered the publisher to pulp it. They destroyed a hundred thousand copies, the day before publication')."

Ellen lost her ability to respond to her boyfriend sexually, and for a time she believed she was frigid. Her boyfriend certainly accused her of being frigid, which is a man's classic (and slanderous) attack on any woman who doesn't want to make love as frequently as he does.

Read My Lips: No Faked Orgasms

There is no such thing as frigidity. There *is* such a thing as an inability (for one reason or another) to have orgasms. But as Dr. Masters said, "Frigidity doesn't mean anything. It means a woman who doesn't orgasm, and it means a woman who has an orgasm once a week and her husband thinks she ought to have it twice. As far as I'm concerned, it's slang, and poor slang. Some male who thinks of women only as sex objects must have affixed it because it is not a term that a woman would apply to a variation of her own response."

Ellen's sexual problem was not that she was unresponsive; or even that she was unwilling to have sex whenever her boyfriend wanted her to. Her sexual problem was that she was not aroused by a man who had no confidence in his own identity.

Of course, if she wanted to continue having a sexual relationship with him, she had a responsibility either to seek professional guidance or to try to analyze her negative reaction and clearly explain it to him, and tell him that it was an issue that would make or break their future relationship. Honesty and forthrightness are absolutely essential for the achievement of peak-performance sex. Read my lips: No faked orgasms.

Some sexual difficulties that women face can be comparatively minor. One woman found that she was becoming increasingly exasperated with her lover because he was so sloppy and disorganized. She would find his dirty socks under the bed where he had tossed them in the heat of the moment, and "while I'd enjoyed the heat of the moment, the memory of it was kind of marred by finding a stone-cold pair of sweaty socks under the bed about nine days later."

Several women have begun to exhibit negative sexual responses to their husbands as they approached middle-age, because they started to behave so predictably. "I can predict to the second when he's going to put down his paper, yawn, stretch, and say 'How about a nice malted milk before we bed down?' Sometimes I thank God that we don't have an ax in the house, because if we did I think I'd bury it right in the top of his head."

These are problems that may seem trivial, but which need to be resolved before a couple can even think of achieving peak-performance sex together.

Younger women can have fundamental sexual difficulties, as well—difficulties that may well be rooted in their family background and their mother's perception of sex. Here's Debbie, 24, a hair stylist from Santa Fe: "I always thought that my mother was very open and honest about sex. She discussed it without embarrassment, and when I told my friends about her they were all real envious. The problem was that my mother's ideas about sex were so old-fashioned. She seriously didn't think that a woman had any sexuality of her own, but that she was only there to satisfy the man's needs. She kept saying things like, 'Men need it two or three times a week and you have to give it to them.' So the result was that when I first slept with a boy I knew what to do, I knew all about penises and vaginas and wearing a rubber. But I behaved as if it was doing my duty. I didn't think about myself . . . or if *I* was enjoying it. I just lay there while he messed around and poked me about and jumped up and down and I thought 'God, this is so awful, do I really have to put up with this two or three times a week? I'd rather stay single. I'd rather be a nun.' During the whole of those early relationships, I never once experienced an orgasm—but none of my boyfriends seemed to question it. As long as *they* were enjoying themselves, as long as *they* were satisfied, they seemed to assume that everything was all right."

Debbie was lucky, and eventually found a boyfriend who helped her to understand that she had a sexuality of her own—and that she was entitled to expect to be sexually stimulated in ways that were "both personally exciting and acceptable."

Peak-performance sex needs high sexual tension. As Dr. Masters remarked: "A highly excited man is certainly capable of bringing a highly excited woman to orgasm without thinking about how he is doing it, but if the woman feels no sexual tension, his excitement alone will not be enough."

Debbie was devastated when her new boyfriend kissed and caressed her, and then suddenly stopped. "I said, 'What's wrong? What's the matter?' He said, 'Aren't you enjoying this?' I was baffled. I didn't really understand what he meant. I said, 'Sure I'm enjoying it.' But he said, 'Well, why don't you tell your body that you're enjoying it?'

"That evening, Mark began to teach me what my mother should have taught me—that a woman has a sexual personality of her own, that she has her own needs, the same way that men do. He taught me that making love is a partnership, not a service that women provide for horny men.

"The most incredible thing that happened that evening was that Mark went down on me, and licked my vagina. I was frightened. I was so darn frightened! My mother had told me that men sometimes like to kiss a woman *intimately* as she called it, but she'd made it sound as if it was something I would have to suffer—you know, shutting my eyes and sticking my fingers in my ears and humming "Hail To The Chief" until it was all over.

"Instead, it was the most delicate, erotic, intimate thing that had ever happened to me.

"We were lying on a thick blanket on the floor in front of the fire. We were drinking red wine and listening to Van Morrison. Mark kissed my lips, and then kissed my breasts, and then he kissed me all the way down my sides and my stomach. His kisses made me shiver in a way that I'd never shivered before.

"He gently opened my thighs. I guess I knew then what he was going to do but I couldn't really believe that it was happening to me. He ran his tongue all the way down the lips of my vagina and it gave me such a strange exciting feeling. Then he opened up my lips with his fingers, and stuck his tongue right into my open vagina, and licked it and massaged it.

"He opened my legs even wider. I looked down and I could see him flicking his tongue all around my clitoris. I was so tense that I was like a spring, and I guess he could sense it, because he looked up at me and said, 'Relax . . . just enjoy it. I'm not going to hurt you.'

"So I lay back on the blanket and let it happen. His tongue probed just about everywhere, as if he wanted to know everything about me. He licked all the way down the cleft of my bottom and tongued my anus. I never would have dreamed that any man would do that to you . . . let alone that it would feel so erotic. He plunged his tongue back into my vagina, and sucked at my vaginal lips, and then went back to flicking my clitoris.

"I looked down again. His lips and his cheeks were shining wet in the firelight, and so were the insides of my thighs. I wanted him to make love to me then, I wanted his penis inside me, I wanted it badly; but he kept on licking me and licking me and then I felt this huge warm wave beginning to wash over me. Suddenly I felt like I was flying apart . . . I literally felt like I was exploding. It wasn't until it was all over that I realized I had experienced an orgasm like no orgasm that I had ever experienced before.

"I'd *had* orgasms before. I'd masturbated a few times when I was younger, especially when I was reading a sexy book. Judith Krantz books always used to turn me on. But the orgasms I'd had then were totally different . . . sort of quiet, if you know what I mean. This was the first orgasm that I'd shared with somebody else, shared with a man. It wasn't so much like satisfying myself as *expressing* myself. Expressing my sexuality, expressing my needs, and expressing the way I felt about Mark, too."

Few men take kindly to criticism of their sexual performance, and so it is often difficult for a woman to achieve the peak satisfaction of which she is potentially capable. Of all the day-to-day sexual problems that I encounter, lack of basic sexual knowledge and lack of basic lovemaking skills are the most common—and the most difficult to correct.

Many men know a lot about sexual variations such as oral sex and bondage and group sex, but when it comes down to handling and arousing the woman they love, they have only the vaguest ideas about how to touch, how to kiss, how to caress, how to keep up sustained stimulation, and how to make sure that their partner reaches the most satisfying climax possible.

It's not their fault. The plain fact is that nobody has ever shown them how to do it. So many women complain about the speed, the roughness, and the peremptory way in which the men in their lives make love to them—and so many men are surprised and hurt when they eventually discover that they're not very good in bed.

If a woman isn't pleased and satisfied by her lover's sexual technique, then it's up to her to show him how to make love the way she likes it most. Notice that I said *show* rather than *tell*. This is because *telling* a man that he isn't doing it right can cause considerable anger and hurt, and unnecessarily jeopardize a relationship that may, for the most part, be very good.

When, for instance, do you tell him? Just before he's about to make love? If you do it then, you'll only succeed in inhibiting him, or in causing an argument at a moment when both of you are in a high state of sexual and emotional tension. If you do it during lovemaking, you'll probably find that he will lose both his confidence and his erection, and your lovemaking will remain unfinished.

If you tell him *after* you've made love, he'll (rightly) demand to know why you didn't tell him before.

Do you tell him over dinner? While walking down the street? When you wake up in the morning?

From twenty years of experience of assisting women with sexually clumsy or sexually ignorant partners, I must admit that there really is no ideal time to broach the subject of his inadequacy.

In the end, if he fails to take the hint when you show him how you like to make love, you may have to come right out with it. But the most diplomatic way is usually to hand him a book such as this one and say, "Do you know something . . . it says in this book that if you touch a woman's clitoris like this, et cetera, et cetera . . . I didn't know that, did you? Maybe we should try it."

I'm being simplistic. Obviously you know the man in your life better than I do. But almost all men are touchy about their sexual prowess, and for your own satisfaction and sexual well-being, it's better not to undermine their confidence. If you make your partner feel that he can't please you in bed, then you're taking the first step to making him impotent, and that's the very last thing you want.

When he makes love to you, it isn't difficult to ensure that his kisses linger longer. Hold his face in your hands and carry on kissing, even when it's obvious that he wants to get on with fucking. If you show him that his kisses arouse you, then he'll be more aware of them. Fight back with your lips and your tongue. Try trapping his tongue between your teeth (not too hard). Kiss him back. Nip his neck and give him hickeys (not above collar-level, if he works in an office, and not at all if he's married—and by that I mean married to somebody else. One hickey could be a death warrant to your relationship).

Make sure that he takes time caressing your breasts. It's remarkable how many men start love-making by thrusting their hand or their tongue directly between their lover's legs, and completely ignore her breasts—even when she may be exceptionally well-endowed.

You can slow down the proceedings by holding your breasts for him to kiss, first one and then the other, and by caressing his face and his body with your nipples. Remember that in order to get the lovemaking you like best at the *pace* you prefer, you will have to be active and very obviously responsive. In fact, there is no harm in acting a little during foreplay—exaggerating how turned-on you are by breathing a little more heavily and moaning and murmuring your approval.

Your lover isn't psychic, any more than you are, and he simply won't know how much you like your breasts caressed or *how* you like them caressed unless you make it obvious to him. Men tend to be sexually slow on the uptake, so make sure that he really gets the message, either by ummming and aaahhing when he sucks and titillates your nipples, or by saying something like, "Ohh . . . I love it when you squeeze my breasts/suck my nipples/flick with my nipples like that."

There are many ways in which you can delay penetration and ensure that he gives you all the foreplay you need to get really worked up. You can simply hold his penis in your hand, and slowly massage it. He won't complain, and you can make sure that you guide it away from your vagina until you're ready for it.

You can slide down underneath him (or slide down on top of him, or next to him, or wherever you happen to be) and massage his penis between your breasts. If you gently stretch the opening in the head of his penis, you'll find that one of your erect nipples will fit inside it. That's something he won't have thought of doing, and something he'll remember you for.

You can give him oral sex. I have never known a man who refused oral sex as part of foreplay. You don't have to think about fellating him to a climax—just lick and kiss his penis, and take it into your mouth. If you wish to *speed up* his arousal, you can gently suck the head of his penis while quickly flicking it just below the opening with the tip of your tongue. If you wish to *delay* his arousal, you can gently suck the side of the shaft like a corncob, although you can fine-tune the intensity of the sensations you give him according to whether you suck close to the head (more sensitive) or close to the base (less sensitive). You can arouse him a tad more, for example, by licking around the groove that separates the head of his penis from the shaft.

You can pleasurably delay intercourse even longer by fondling his testicles or taking them into your mouth and (gently!!) rolling them around with your tongue. Don't suck them too hard or you will cause him intense and lasting pain, which won't do anything to improve your lovemaking.

During this time, you can ensure that *he* is continuing to stimulate *you* by placing yourself in a position where he can easily reach your breasts and your vagina. If you decide to give him oral sex, for example, you can either kneel beside him, with your calf against his arm, or you can actually sit astride his chest with your vagina within licking distance of his tongue. This is the famous position known as "soixante-neuf" because you and he form the figure 69 between you. (A rather plump friend of mine admitted that when he and his wife enjoyed mutual oral sex, it was more like "88" than "69.")

14

A Lady's Guide to Peak Performance

You can see now that a woman can exert a remarkable amount of control over the way in which she and her lover have sex *without him feeling that he has lost his male dominance*. In the context of sexual relationships, I don't use the phrase "male dominance" in the sense of a woman being a man's sexual plaything, to treat as he likes. But for purely psychosexual reasons that bear no relation to the way in which a man and a woman should interact with each other in their everyday lives, a man is sexually driven by the urge to penetrate his lover with his penis and to show her that he is strong and virile and capable of satisfying her. It's his caveman instinct, and it's a very important part of what arouses him, and what keeps him hard. That's why, in counseling, I always place so much emphasis on a woman *showing* and *guiding* her lover rather than telling him or (heaven forbid) nagging or belittling him, which too many women do.

If you criticize a man's lovemaking, you'll only create new problems and make the situation worse than it was before. But if you *show* and *guide* and *respond* (even if some of it's feminine play-acting) you should eventually begin to enjoy the skills of a lover who really knows how to please you.

Don't expect to achieve a brand-new sex life over-night. Old habits die hard, and old sexual habits die harder than most. Apart from lack of skill and lack of knowledge, another common male failing is sex-ual laziness—most typically in long-lasting mar-riages and long-term relationships. Now that the thrill of the chase has worn off, and his woman doesn't have to be dragged into bed by her hair every night, our caveman loses interest in lovemak-ing and devotes his attention to work, golf, and six-packs instead. It isn't only women who avoid lovemaking by having "headaches" and being too tired.

But a sexually lazy man can be aroused if you introduce something new and stimulating into his moribund routine. Try one or more of the following *tonight* and see what happens:

1. Climb into the tub or the shower with him, and massage him with a fragrant new bath or shower gel.
2. Bring in an ice-cold bottle of champagne instead of warm milk, and tell him you're celebrating the anniversary of the first time you made love (or—if he's one of those rare men who can remember the date when you really did make love for the first time—tell him it's the anniver-sary of the first time he gave you a multiple orgasm. He sure as hell won't know *that!*).
3. If you usually wear a nightgown, go to bed nude, or wear nothing but a bra that bares your nipples, or one of Frederick of Holly-wood's best see-through fluffy trimmed baby-doll numbers. Or a pair of open-crotch panties.

On the subject of erotic clothing, it's important to wear whatever makes *you* feel sexy as well as something that you know turns your man on. If you feel embarrassed or unsure of yourself in your purple satin G-string, then don't wear it. Your uncertainty will convey itself to your lover, and not only could you lose the sexy mood, but you could make things very awkward. Some men are embarrassed that erotic underwear turns them on, and will react negatively to their partner if she tries to "spring" it on them as a surprise. "I couldn't understand it," said 31-year-old Jennie, from Springfield, Massachusetts, who had attempted to arouse her sexually somnolent husband by wearing a long white topless satin nightgown. "I thought it was erotic, but it was elegant, too. But Bill totally lost his temper and said I looked like a whore. It was only much later that he said he was sorry, and said he'd like to see me wearing it again. I guess he was embarrassed because it excited him. He hadn't expected to see his own boring old wife looking so sexy."

My advice is that if a woman feels at all hesitant about wearing erotic underwear—if she's embarrassed, or worried that her lover may think she's cheap, then she shouldn't attempt to wear it as a bedtime surprise. Again, it could be a threat to that precious male sexual dominance—the fact that *you* made the first and most obvious move. A woman can certainly attract her man by wearing sexier lingerie, and there are scores of catalogs that offer all kinds of highly erotic outfits. But some women find that it's better if they simply buy it and start wearing it without making a fuss about it. Norma, for example, a 27-year-old secretary from Buffalo, New York, ordered a selection of G-strings and briefs (including a black ciré pair with a zipper all the way from the front to the back) and a black fishnet cat suit. She started to wear them as a matter of course, and within three days claimed "my sex life had suddenly taken off."

Most catalogs of erotic lingerie also contain "fantasy uniforms"—sexual play outfits such as nurses' or waitresses' costumes. Heidi, a buxom 44-year-old housewife from Indianapolis, bought herself a nurse's outfit because her second husband George had mentioned on several occasions how much he had enjoyed his time in hospital after he had crushed his ankle in a trucking accident "because of the way those nurses took care of me. They did everything for me, and I mean everything." Although George had not said so in so many words, Heidi assumed that the nurses had either given him manual sexual relief from time to time, or else he had strongly fantasized about it. Either way, she knew that he was aroused by nurses, and she decided to play the part for herself.

"The outfit was only thirty-five dollars, and as far as I'm concerned it was the best thirty-five dollars I'd spent in years. There was a small white cap with a red cross on it, a very short button-through uniform in white wet-look satin, and a red wet-look apron. I wore white hold-up stockings underneath it, and white tennis shoes.

"It was quite late. George was lying in bed, working on some papers. I came out of the bathroom carrying a warm wet facecloth and a towel, and I said, 'Okay, George, time for your bath.' He laughed, but he was delighted. I took his papers away from him and laid him down flat. Then I unbuttoned his pajamas and washed his face and his chest, and dried him. His erection was so big that it came right out of the fly of his pajama pants. I didn't touch it at first, but made sure that I kept accidentally-on-purpose flicking it with my apron or my towel or my arm.

"He tried to grab me but I slapped his hand away and told him, 'Don't . . . I'm the nurse and I'm in charge.' I loosened his pajama pants and washed his cock, rubbing it very, very slowly up and down. He was panting like he'd been jogging or something! Then finally I climbed on top of him, and lifted my uniform. I had shaved my pubic hair for the first time ever, and that blew George's mind. He had an erection so hard that I thought he was going to burst. I said, 'Tonight we have to give you a special personal treatment,' and I guided his erection up into my vagina, and rode up and down on him at just the speed I wanted, at just the right angle to make my vagina feel fantastic.

"What was good about it was that I was doing something which turned George on, but at the same time I was able to make love in exactly the way I needed it. George was usually far too rough, and far too quick. But that night I went up and down, up and down, as slow and gentle as I wanted. George fondled my breasts through my uniform, rubbing my nipples through the satin, and that turned me on even more. In the end, the patient got better, and I mean better. He rolled me over onto my back, and lifted my stockinged legs over his shoulders, and he fucked me so deep that I can remember screaming. I had two-and-a-half orgasms, one after the other. Two huge ones and then a little one. Then George took out his erection and shot what felt like gallons of warm sperm all over my shaved vagina, and slowly massaged it in, and I had about a hundred little muscle spasms—*very* pleasurable, almost *too* pleasurable.

"I told a close friend of mine that I had dressed up like a nurse to turn George on. I think she was pretty shocked, although she tried not to show it. She seemed to think that it was wrong to do something like that to please your husband. But I know for a fact how dull *her* sex life is; and I also know for a fact that I got just as much satisfaction out of dressing up like that as George did.

"I still put on the uniform occasionally . . . maybe once a month, once every eight weeks. It's more exciting if you don't overdo it. And that's the only time I shave myself, too, so George always knows that he has something extra to look forward to, when I lift up that little short dress."

I spoke with other women who had dressed up in anything from white lace to black leather, depending on their lovers' tastes (and their own). Katie, a 28-year-old photographer from Lansing, Michigan, bought herself a black leather basque that left her breasts bare, and was attached between the legs with a single, thin, black leather strap, "buckled very tight, so that it completely disappears into my pussy," black leather thigh boots, black leather elbow-length gloves, and black leather straps that buckled her wrists only 6 inches apart and her ankles only a foot apart. She had taken dozens of photographs of herself dressed in this outfit, and then wore it for her 32-year-old boyfriend, Jim. She puts it on only occasionally. "You don't need sex of that kind of intensity all the time . . . you'd quickly get to a point where you needed things that were really extreme, and neither of us has much of an interest in taking our sex lives into heavy bondage or heavy fetishism. But when I *do* wear it, it turns him on like crazy. He says it's like seeing a sexual side of me that's not quite his to own. It makes him understand that I'm an individual, that I have my own sexual identity—that I'm not just an extension of him. I like him to buckle my wrists to the top of the bed, and my ankles to the foot of the bed, and then he can do anything he wants to me, and I'm powerless to stop him. I find it frightening but I also find it very exciting. Of course you have to have a high degree of trust in somebody to get into that kind of sex with them, but I trust Jim—even though he likes to surprise me sometimes. Once he bought these two huge vibrators. I still have them someplace. They're kind of semitransparent and they're made of this jellylike plastic and they have dozens of little balls inside them which kind of churn around when you switch them on. He slicked them up with lubricant, and then he slid one of them up my pussy and forced the other one up my behind. Then he put them on top speed and left them inside me, and there was nothing I could do to get them out. He kept on kissing me, and kissing my breasts, and after about five minutes I climaxed, and then again, and then again, and in the end I had to *beg* him to take them out. It was too much. Another time he brought in a young German shepherd with a studded collar on, and got the dog to lick me between the legs. That was terrifying, but I got an incredible rush out of it, too, and the dog sure didn't object. A vet told me later that quite a few women actually *train* their dogs to do it."

Of course I'm not suggesting that you necessarily need to explore the fringes of unusual sex to find peak satisfaction. But as I've said so many times before, if a sexual activity stimulates you both, and you both enjoy it (even if one of you enjoys it more than the other), and it does you no physical harm, then there need be no limit to what you do. It's your body; your life; and there's no need to be anxious or ashamed about trying anything and everything that sexually excites you.

After that short diversion, let's get back to those things you can do tonight.

4. As soon as you climb into bed, slide down and start kissing his penis. If he asks you what's happening, tell him you're having a midnight feast.

5. Rent or buy a good-quality hardcore video, and put it on the TV. If you don't have a TV in the bedroom, buy some hardcore magazines instead. Shopping for porn might take a little nerve, but the results (on your lover) can be spectacular.

Deep Throat and *Debbie Does Dallas* and *The Devil in Miss Jones* are looking distinctly old-fashioned these days, especially because their stars are now respectable middle-aged women. But among several extremely erotic new videos available today is *Health Spa*, with Abigail Clayton and Kay Parker—"set in the hottest fitness center ever . . . the main program is 'sexercise,' a real sexy workout of masturbation and fucking." Then there's Traci Duzit and Fawn Paris in *Cherry Busters*—"see Mindy perform lesbian acts with her beautiful girlfriend, who later takes three men at once, losing control of herself in screaming ecstasy while three pricks ram into her simultaneously." Or the "Foxy Lady" series starring the very remarkable Teresa Orlowski—at more than $200 per cassette, one of the most expensive sex-video series on the market—"the ultimate in erotica, Teresa has beauty, the most gorgeous body with the most exquisite large breasts that you will ever see . . . she just loves sex with three or four men at once . . . pricks up her ass, cunt and mouth at the same time are what she craves . . . or a wine bottle up her cunt and a prick in her ass." Some videos cater to even more extreme tastes. Although many people may not find them especially arousing—and some people may even find them distasteful—I have discovered that couples whose relationships have been suffering from a lack of creativity and a lack of sexual imagination have often broadened their sexual thinking by watching extreme-sex movies. At the very least, it has helped to loosen their sexual inhibitions. But on several occasions, a man and a woman have discovered that one or the other of them has been keeping a strong sexual urge deeply repressed, in the belief that it was "kinky" or "dirty," and that nobody else in the world shared or would tolerate such urges. Sometimes *both* of them have shared the same repressed urge, and are astonished to find that they have been living together for weeks or months or even years without realizing it.

So even if you're not thinking of renting or buying an extreme-sex video, it's worthwhile taking a look at the catalogs to see if any particular sexual variation arouses your curiosity. Bear in mind that just because you or your partner (or both of you) are aroused by watching an extreme sexual act, that doesn't mean that you're sexually kinky yourself, or that either of you is under any obligation to try the acts that you see on the screen. You can be thrilled by a sky-diving movie without having the urge to immediately fling yourself out of an airplane.

There are some *very* odd videos available—such as *Bizarre Special*: "a Lilliputian, a fat girl with very big breasts, a tattooed punk girl and a very tall one—all playing an extreme sex game." But otherwise they tend to fall into specific categories relating to well-known sexual variations. There are numerous videos depicting anal sex—such as *Caught From Behind IV*: "backed up with a talented cast of the most beautiful sex-hungry ladies, Rambone and his incredible 15½ inches of anal-penetrating pleasure." There are a very few movies about fist-fucking, in which women are vaginally and anally penetrated by a man's entire hand. But there are many more concerned with bondage—like *A Woman's Mind*: "Jan is rich and powerful but she only comes sexually alive when she is helplessly bound and gagged." And a remarkable number starring women who are heavily pregnant or lactating—*The Milky Way*, for instance, which "features four actresses who get off on revealing their swollen milk-engorged breasts . . . and milk isn't the only fluid that runs in torrents"—or *Unwed Mothers*: "the secret desires of pregnant girls in a lactating lesbian orgy."

There are videos featuring men with unbelievably huge penises; women with unbelievably huge breasts; women having sex with dogs, pigs, and donkeys; men having sex with each other; women having sex with each other; pubic shaving; wet sex and enemas; transvestites; transexuals and "she-males." Whatever sexual variation you can think of, there's a video about it.

If you accept these videos for what they are: erotic entertainment—a completely harmless way of exciting and arousing you—then both you and your man can derive a great deal of sexual pleasure from them. You're a mature and responsible adult, so they won't corrupt you, they won't poison you, and they won't harm the rain forests or the ozone layer. They can be an education, too, and they can help some couples to make love with much less inhibition.

Here's Nadine, a 24-year-old homemaker from Tucson, Arizona: "I was pregnant with my first child at the age of nineteen. I knew where babies came from, of course, but I was very ignorant about sex altogether. My mother said that you should never have sex when you're pregnant in case the man's penis hits the fetus on the head and gives it brain damage. She also said that the reason a woman swelled up so much, her breasts and everything, was to make her less attractive to her husband during pregnancy so that he wouldn't feel like making love to her so much.

"So what happened was that I refused to let Ray touch me, from the moment the clinic told me I was expecting. I just wouldn't let him go anywhere near me. I didn't think that he really wanted to. When he said I looked beautiful I thought he was just trying to be nice to me. I surely didn't want a brain-damaged child, either.

"He Adored Her Being Pregnant"

"But then I was talking to a friend of mine over coffee and she said that her husband had seen me a couple of days before, and was really keen for *her* to get pregnant again—not that she was going to, no way. I said I hadn't realized that her husband liked kids so much. She said he didn't—he just adored her when she was pregnant. He liked her big breasts and her big round stomach, and the thought that he was making love to the woman he loved with his own child inside her was a major turn-on.

"Of course, after what my mom had told me, I was astonished. But Lara said that there was nothing wrong with having sex when you were pregnant, provided you weren't too violent about it, and provided your doctor said it was okay. She said that Mike was so turned on by the pregnant look that he'd bought a couple of sex videos with pregnant girls in them. I told Ray about it that evening when he came home from work. First of all he was angry at my mom for having told me such an old wives' tale. Then he was angry at me for having believed it. Then he laughed about the whole thing. He'd really believed that I was going through some kind of hormone problem, now that I was pregnant, and that I'd gone off sex completely.

"Anyway, the next morning Lara came around, and brought the videos with her. That evening, Ray and I went to bed early and we watched them. We'd watched a video called *Desires Within Young Girls* once, just before we were married, but that was the only sex video I'd ever seen. I'm not prudish or anything. I actually *like* sexy movies—provided I can watch them with Ray. But these two movies were something else.

"In the first one, there were two very young girls, both of them seven or eight months' pregnant, and they were each being screwed by two men at once. Then, when the men had finished with them, they took turns licking each other's pussies. There was one scene where the girls are both lying on the bed, head to toe. One girl climbs on top of the other girl, so that both of their huge swollen stomachs are pressed together . . . then the girl lying on the bed opens up the cheeks of the other girl's ass, and great blobs of sperm slide out of her pussy and her ass, onto the first girl's breasts. The first girl squeezes her breasts, so that you can see the colostorum dripping out of her nipples. Then she massages it all together, sperm and colostorum, and the girl who's on top of her turns around and sucks and licks her nipples until she's sucked it all up. I think that was pretty extreme, yes, and I sure wouldn't make love to two men at once, *or* another girl. But it was a big turn-on to watch it, and it did encourage Ray and me to go on making love . . . right until the seventh month.

"After that it got kind of uncomfortable, but Ray still used to go down on me once or twice a week, so that I got plenty of sexual satisfaction. He enjoyed licking me out because my pussy was so swollen, and the lips were so fat, and I had even more juice than usual. My whole stomach used to go hard as a rock when I had an orgasm, and the baby used to kick like crazy. But she was born healthy and happy, and I'm not surprised, with healthy and happy parents.''

Obviously, your doctor or midwife will advise you if there is any risk attached to continuing sexual intercourse during your pregnancy. But there is no possible danger of your lover's penis injuring your baby (although it's probably advisable to give up vibrators for the time being), and lovemaking during a normal pregnancy is not only desirable but good for your general well-being.

Remember that, for a man, his partner's pregnancy is almost always a time of great sexual pride and self-satisfaction. As he escorts her around, she is displaying public proof that he has made love to her, and that she is happy to carry his child.

6. And, the last thing you can do tonight is to put your arms around him in the wee small hours, and slowly begin to massage his penis. Then, enjoy the consequences. You'd be surprised how many men like to be woken up before cock-crow.

You will have noticed that each of these six suggestions calls on women to display much more initiative in their sexual relationships than they might have been used to. They require a high degree of sexual self-education; a high degree of sexual tolerance; and a willingness to venture into areas of erotic experience that many women might have considered to be kinky, strange, or even frightening.

But I cannot overemphasize the importance of a

woman's role in staking out the length and breadth of a sexual relationship. Within limits, men are prepared to try almost anything in their search for sexual sensation. Ask any man whether he would like his lover to give him more or less oral sex, more or less anal sex, more or fewer sexual variations. Then ask any woman the same questions, and you will quickly conclude (as I have done, over the years) that, as a rule, it is the woman's inhibitions (or lack of them) that draw a couple's sexual parameters.

Ultimately, it is the woman's enthusiasm for sexual satisfaction that will determine whether or not a couple can reach the very peaks of sexual pleasure. Although the man plays a physically dominant role, the woman (by her response to him) sets the underlying tone, and the longer a relationship continues, the more *her* feelings about sex will affect their everyday lovemaking.

Is she shy, inhibited, and cautious? Does she enjoy sex or is she afraid of it? Is she sexually withdrawn, suffering his attentions in silence? Or does she openly display a strong feminine passion, and a willingness to enjoy all of the sensual pleasures that the sexual attraction between two people can provide?

If a woman is sexually knowledgeable, she will be sexually confident: and if she is sexually confident, she will be able to explore the limits of her own passion without fear, and at her own pace. One of the most critical aspects of achieving peak-performance sex is for a couple to be able to close what sexologists call "the arousal gap."

As one sex researcher remarked: "One fact of human sexuality that has come over most clearly is that most men are easily aroused by purely physical, bodily stimuli; whereas a woman's full sexual response depends far more on her state of mind and on her total responsiveness to her partner. The initial stages of arousal are more immediate for a man and can be triggered by fewer stimuli—the sight of a nipple or perhaps a thigh or, for our grandfathers, even an ankle."

What I find interesting, however, is that women who are sexually knowledgeable and sexually confident become sexually aroused almost as quickly as men, and are therefore able to reach the peaks of sexual pleasure far more rapidly than their less knowledgeable and confident sisters. The comparative slowness with which many women become sexually aroused seems to be more related to their mental attitude toward sex and their social conditioning than it is to their physical and emotional ability to enjoy "a good fuck."

Masters' and Johnson's research into human sexual response bears this out. They were the first researchers to analyze in detail the physical changes taking place within both partners during intercourse, and what was remarkable about their results was not how different men and women are physically—but how similar.

Let's take a look now at a woman's sexual organs, and what happens to them during sexual excitement and orgasm; and, at the same time, let's see how she can teach her lover to touch her the way she likes best, and what both he and she can do to bring her to the most ecstatic orgasm possible.

Although a woman's ability to bear children has always made it obvious that her vagina is very elastic, the complex functioning of a woman's sexual organs remained a mystery for hundreds of years. Physiologists simply didn't know what went on inside a woman's body, and perhaps there was also a disinclination to find out. Historically and mythologically, men have always been slightly fearful of the female vagina, as well as attracted to it.

It is only in the past quarter of a century that physiologists and therapists have begun to understand the complex functioning of a woman's sexual organs during intercourse, and even more recently that they have learned how best to use that understanding in order to make sure that women enjoy sex to the utmost.

We have already discussed the external female sex organs—her vulva—and identified her outer and inner lips, her clitoris, her urethra, and the vestibule of her vagina.

I've always regretted that the words to describe some of the most desirable and beautiful parts of a woman's body are either crude and semi-obscene or pompous and archaic. *Vulva* is actually Latin for "womb," so it's inaccurate as well as being overly scientific. *Cunt*, too, is Old English for "womb," and is related to the Norse word *kunte*. Perhaps the most romantic words for the female sexual organs or *mindj* or *minsh*, which are derived from the Romany. Perhaps the gypsies knew how to make love to their women more ardently than the Romans or the Old English.

When a woman is sexually aroused, her inner lips (the *labia minora*) swell up to three times their normal size, and protrude beyond the outer lips (the *labia majora*). Any woman will be able to see this change quite clearly for herself if she masturbates or makes love in front of a mirror or video camera. Her inner lips also change color, sometimes quite dramatically, from pink or brownish-pink to bright red or a deep wine color.

During the early stages of sexual arousal, your lover might be tempted immediately to start stimulating your clitoris. Men know about clitorides these days, but many men unfortunately regard them as a kind of pushbutton that will immediately arouse a woman and ensure that they reach orgasm. In fact, one of the most common descriptions of the clitoris in sex fiction and slang is "love-button."

This is Rhoda, a 24-year-old research assistant from St. Louis, describing a sexual encounter she had with her 33-year-old boss after he had taken her out to dinner: "He drove me home and asked me if he could come up to my apartment for coffee or maybe a drink. I said no. I knew that my roommate was already home and that the situation wouldn't be comfortable. Besides, this was our first date and, although I was very attracted to him, I wasn't at all sure that I wanted to go to bed with him.

"He tried to persuade me to invite him inside, but when he was convinced that I wasn't going to give in, he said, okay, then, at least give me a goodnight kiss. I didn't object to that because I did like him a lot.

"He kissed me and he was very good at kissing. He fondled my breasts through my dress, and he slipped his hand into my bra and played with my nipples. Then he started running his hand up inside my skirt. I didn't actually resist, no, because I was enjoying it, and I liked him. He touched my panties, and he said, 'You're all wet,' and I was; but I guess that was just a compliment to how good he kissed.

"But then he pulled my panties to one side and started fingering me—quite hard, and quite roughly—at least it felt that way. I told him to quit but he wouldn't. In the end I had to pull his hand out and push him away. He was pretty sore about it. He said, 'What's the matter with you? Are you frigid or something?'

"Well—isn't that exactly the defense that all men come up with, when they've made a fool of themselves? I wasn't frigid. I was the opposite of frigid. I was all ready to make love to him then and there, in the front seat of the car, if he'd wanted me to. But he rubbed my clitoris like he was sandpapering a barn, and it *hurt*. That was all I was telling him: back off a little, you're rubbing too hard, and all you're doing is turning me *off* when I'm already turned *on*.

"The trouble was, he couldn't accept the fact that he wasn't a lovemaking expert, and instead of letting me show him how to do it the way I liked it, he got angry. I said to him, 'Don't get crazy, don't get crazy, let me show you.' But he wouldn't. All he said was, 'I've heard about girls like you. You're all dykes, when it comes down to it, dykes."

But our boss from the office was wrong. Rhoda wasn't a lesbian, and she certainly wasn't frigid. As I've said before, "frigidity" has no physiological or psychosexual meaning; it is usually used as an insult by men who have failed to arouse a woman as quickly and as dramatically as they thought their virility merited.

The fact is that a woman's clitoris is crammed with nerve fibers. Among these fibers are microscopic structures called Pacinian corpuscles, which are highly sensitive to pressure. The tip of the clitoris (the glans) has more nerve fibers than any other part of the vulva, and the Pacinian corpuscles are even closer together, so that the touch of a man's finger will send a torrent of nerve signals to his partner's brain.

But touching a woman's clitoris is not the same as touching a man's penis. A woman's clitoral response is very much slower. Whereas a man's penis enlarges at the first indication of his sexual excitement, the equivalent reaction in a woman's clitoris occurs later—*after* the first lubricating juice has been secreted by her vagina. Direct rubbing of a woman's clitoris, especially the tip of the clitoris, is not a recommended technique at the very beginning of sexual stimulation. Any man who tries to push the "love-button" in so immediate and direct a manner will probably end up with the same response that Rhoda gave to her boss.

It makes much more sense for a man to take the time to kiss a woman as if he means it, to fondle and stimulate her breasts as if he adores them, to run his hands over her body and her thighs, and only *then* to think about touching her vulva. More than 80 percent of the women with whom I discussed the subject of clitoral stimulation agreed. The most common complaint: "I feel like he's learned from this manual of sex—and this manual said 'the center of a woman's sexual response is her clitoris'—so he rubs away at the clitoris like it's his cock or something, and all he succeeds in doing is making me feel *scratched*, and irritable."

The preferred touch: "I like it when he strokes all around my cunt . . . when he tugs and tangles my pubic hair . . . when he runs his finger very gently down the whole cleft . . . then gently opens my lips. I like it when he caresses me all around the entrance to my vagina, sometimes slipping the tip of his finger inside, gently opening my vagina wider so that I feel like I'm exposed to him . . . even the inside of my body completely bare for him to look at, and touch, and enjoy. I like it when he strokes my cunt-lips, so softly that it's almost like he's kissing me; gentle fingertips and soft flesh. I like it when he strokes the shaft of my clitoris, slowly at first, and so delicately that I can scarcely feel it, those downward butterfly caresses . . . then gradually growing stronger, and quicker . . . stretching my cunt-lips wider and wider with his fingers so that my clitoris sticks out . . . and flicking the shaft and the tip so quickly and sweetly that I can scarcely feel it . . . but there's something deep inside of me that's growing and growing . . . and when it's fully grown, it's going to blossom out like a huge dark flower and I'm going to be completely carried away . . ."

That description is a compilation of tape-recorded responses from more than twenty-five different women and girls to a question I asked them: *Tell me, in your own words, how you best like your lover to touch your vulva.*

You will notice that over and over again women use the words *gently* and *softly.* They appreciate a man whose penis is fully hard—and as intercourse progresses and their passion heightens, they enjoy the feelings of that hard penis being thrust strongly and deeply into their vaginas. But the first intimate caresses should be gentle, teasing, skillful, and provocative.

As Maggie, 39, a cocktail waitress from South Bend, Indiana, told me: "I prefer to be touched too gentle than too rough. Rough is a turn-off. I won't say that there aren't times when I like a man to pick me up in his arms and pull off my panties and fuck me up against a doorway . . . but that's usually with a man I already know well, and I don't certainly don't care for a man to be violent all the time . . . Just because a man touches you gentle doesn't mean that he's weak, no way. He can hold you strong in his arms, but touch you gentle.

"I like it when a man touches me without trying to take my panties off first . . . when he runs his fingertips down the cleft in my panties and between my legs and teases me, you know? I like it when he makes me wet even before he undresses me. Then he can either take my panties off me or just tug them over to one side, so that my cunt's exposed.

Then I like him to hold my whole cunt in his hand like he's holding a peach or something, and run his middle finger gently up and down the cleft, so that my lips gradually open, little by little. A man could do that to me all night and I wouldn't complain.

"Sometimes I feel like having a man's cock inside me real bad, but I'll hold myself in check, because if I hold myself in check then I know that when I *do* get it inside me, I'll enjoy it all the better. I like a man to slide his fingers up inside me before he touches my clit. I like to feel he's exploring me . . . I like to feel that he *wants* to explore me. I love it when a man slides his thumb up my cunt and then slides two fingers up my ass. I love that feeling . . . especially when he massages his thumb against his fingertips, right through that thin slippery skin . . . and gently tugs me, especially when he gets a kind of bossa nova rhythm going (*laughs*).

"I'm Abducted by a Muscly Tartar"

"A lot of men have this idea that all women want to be raped . . . you know, taken by force. A woman can have fantasies about that. I saw a movie about Genghis Khan once, and for a long time afterward I had erotic fantasies about being abducted by a huge sweaty muscly Tartar in a horned helmet—you know, scooped up onto his horse and having to sit behind him with my arms clinging tight around his waist. Then we're riding along and my hands start massaging his huge muscular greasy thighs . . . and all he's wearing is these leather briefs, which expose his balls at the side, and I can slip my hand into his briefs, and massage his balls and his cock. He gets this huge hard-on, about a foot long—greasy and thick, with enormous stand-out veins and a giant plum-red head on it that smells of leather and sweat and piss—and somehow in my fantasy I climb around him and sit on his cock while he's riding. It's so huge that I scream. And of course he's galloping across the plains of wherever-it-is at full speed and this massive greasy cock is going in and out of my cunt with every gallop.

"I come and I come and I'm screaming for him to stop because I can't come anymore, but he won't.

"I mean, this is a very sexy fantasy I used to have and I used to think about it almost every night and invent more and more detail. I mean, even the *smell?* But it's a fantasy, that's all, like a woman's story in a magazine, or one of those historical novels. If it *really* happened to me, I'd hate it. I don't want to fuck any filthy old Tartar, no way. And I think that men have to understand that. They have to learn to separate the things that women fantasize about from what they actually want.

"I'd say women want masculinity, by which I mean decisiveness, and strength, and opinions on things, and a sense of taking care of a woman. But I'd also say that as far as sex is concerned they want skillfulness—a guy who knows what he's doing and doesn't fumble—and also a guy who knows what he wants but takes his time doing it. What's that song by the Pointer Sisters about a man with a slow hand? That's what women like.

"I respect a man's cock. When I touch a man's cock for the first time I don't snatch ahold of it like it's a grab handle in an automobile. I hold it firm but gentle, the way that a man *likes* it, and I stroke it up and down the way that he likes it. When a man first touches my cunt, I expect him to treat it with the same respect. You'd be surprised how many men still don't seem to understand that a woman's cunt isn't a hole for them to stick their dicks in. There's no excuse for them being ignorant. There are plenty of men's magazines which show absolutely everything—lips, clitoris, cunt-hole, asshole, everything. Full color, pin-sharp. Yet when they meet a real woman they seem to think that all they have to do is give her a quick fiddle and then it's in with the dick. When are men going to learn to be *gentle* when they touch their women?"

I have included most of what Maggie had to say about the way men stimulate their partner's sexual organs because it encompassed so many important points—including the fascinating subject of sexual fantasy. The sexual imaginations of both sexes are a theater of highly erotic dramas; but just because we can excite ourselves by watching these plays that go on in our heads, that doesn't necessarily mean that we want to act them out.

Sexual fantasy plays a valuable part in arousing us, and giving our erotic urges shape and form and color. But the mature and educated lover knows that fantasy is fantasy, and that a woman who becomes aroused by reading about a gang-rape would (in reality) be traumatized by such an experience. He can touch and stimulate his woman with all the skill and lightness of touch that she adores, while at the same time using muscular body movements and firm embraces to give her the *impression* of physical strength and sexual domination. (And *please* remember what I said about male sexual domination—it's part of the psychological experience of intercourse, and doesn't necessarily mean that the man has—or seeks—a superior role.)

Vera, a 24-year-old dress designer from Atlanta, Georgia, had repeated fantasies six or seven months after she was married to Bradley, her 32-year-old husband. Bradley was an airline pilot and consequently Vera spent two or three nights of every week alone.

"I began to have fantasies about having a lesbian affair. I think it was partly centered on my games teacher from high school. I used to have a terrible crush on her when I was about fifteen. She had black hair, which she combed back very severely, and a rather Slavic-looking face and absolutely huge breasts. She was very strict, too. I used to imagine what it would be like to get into the shower with her naked and fondle her breasts. It used to excite me quite a lot. Of course nothing ever happened. The games teacher was married to a rather haughty professor of chemistry and I don't suppose she even *looked* at us silly pubescent girls.

"But on nights when Bradley was away on the coast, I began to have fantasies about having a lesbian affair with a woman very much like my games teacher. I imagined a very dominant, very beautiful woman in a black basque and black stockings and stiletto heels. She would have a black stock whip, and if I didn't obey her every word instantly, she would snap me with it. She would make me kiss her breasts and bite her nipples. Then she would kneel astride me and make me give her oral sex, opening up her vagina with her fingers and pressing it against my mouth so that I almost suffocated. If I was slow making her come, she would snap me with the whip some more. By the time she was close to her orgasm, my skin would be crisscrossed with red whip marks. And when she *did* come, she would rub her wet vagina all over my face, so that even my eyelashes were stuck together with juice.

"If she thought that I'd been good, she would deign to force the braided handle of the stock whip up my bottom, as far as it would go, and allow me to crawl around the bedroom on all fours with the whip coming out of my bottom like a long tail.

"I used to masturbate when I had these fantasies, and I always used to reach orgasm, but of course I didn't feel satisfied the way I did with Bradley. Well, not *of course*. I guess you can be satisfied by masturbation, but Bradley's a very good lover. But in the end I started worrying about this fantasy. I didn't think that I was a masochist, and I knew for sure that I wasn't really a lesbian. I *like* other women, for sure, but they simply don't turn me on.

"Eventually I plucked up enough courage to tell Bradley what I'd been fantasizing. I was frightened that he would interpret it all wrong, and think that I was trying to find a way to tell him that I was a lesbian. But he listened—you know, very quiet and sympathetic—and then he shook his head and laughed. He said he had fantasies all the time, when he was away from me. In fact he had a fantasy that was pretty similar to mine. He fantasized that he had to serve at table, stark naked, while all these women in very sexy outfits made him bring them food, and pour them wine, and sometimes they'd take a mouthful of wine, and then insist on taking a mouthful of Bradley's cock.

"We talked the whole thing through. And, do you know, it was obvious to both of us that I wasn't interested in women, or in *really* having a whip pushed up my bottom; and that Bradley wasn't *really* turned on by the idea of waiting on twenty half-naked women. But we shared our fantasies, and that was great. In fact we made love much more passionately afterward than we had before—I guess because we felt closer.

"It's not always easy to tell the person you love and respect about your dirtiest daydreams . . . but you should. The one thing I learned from that experience was that sex is all about sharing.

"Oh—and I still have the same old fantasy. But why not?"

15

The Crucial Clitoris

We have seen that the glans of a woman's clitoris is crowded with sensitive nerve fibers, which can give her intense sexual pleasure—but which, incorrectly and roughly handled, can also give her intense sexual irritation.

The way that a man stimulates his partner's sexual organs in the early stages of intercourse is absolutely critical to the entire sexual experience that he and she are about to share. His touching technique can make all the difference between a memorable and satisfying act of love and a disorganized, half-aroused, poorly timed fuck, which affords both partners no more than the pleasure of having been physically connected.

This is why I believe so strongly in the free and open exposure of one lover's genitals to the other. A woman should be able to touch and look at and stimulate her partner's penis whenever she feels the urge; and in the same way a man ought to be able to examine and touch his partner's vulva.

Lovers should masturbate each other as frequently as they can—not necessarily to orgasm, but in order to discover what feels good and what feels less than good—and what feels downright irritating. I talked to Megan, a 55-year-old homemaker from Vineland, New Jersey, who complained that in 32 years her husband Lyle had never once masturbated her to orgasm. "He never uses his fingers . . . he uses his dick, and that's it. He seems to think that anything else is 'messing around.' "

It's not unusual to find a disinclination among middle-aged lovers to learn the sexual facts that they were never taught when they were younger—and to be hidebound with sexual inhibitions. Neither is it unusual to find that once they've grown older and their children have grown up and left home, they settle into a "no-sex" routine—or, at best, a "sex-once-a-month" routine.

But for the first time, middle-aged lovers have the opportunity to make love whenever they feel like it—and *wherever* they feel like it. What's even more important, they should be close and confident enough, after a long-lasting relationship, to explain both their unfulfilled sexual fantasies and needs to each other.

As men and women grow older, their sexual response slows down, but that doesn't mean that they no longer need the satisfaction and pleasure that a sexual relationship can continue to give them, well into their sixties and seventies. After menopause, many women begin to consider themselves unattractive to their partners, because they can no longer give birth. Men, too, become worried about the time it takes for them to achieve an erection.

But peak-performance sex means doing your very best whatever your age and your capabilities, and mature lovers can derive just as much satisfaction from sex as couples who are forty years younger. It is never too late to learn how to please your partner—and I speak from experience. I have talked to young men of twenty who were unsure about how to touch their lover's sexual organs; and I have also talked to men of fifty who have had the same problem.

What these men shared was the realization that,

if they wanted to satisfy the women in their lives, they had to know how to do it.

There are marked similarities between the clitoris and the penis. When a fetus is developing in its mother's womb, it has a small lump of tissue between its legs even before its sex can be determined. If it turns out to be a boy, that lump of tissue grows into a penis. If it turns out to be a girl, that same lump of tissue remains relatively small and develops into the clitoris.

A woman's clitoris has no opening, like a man's penis. But in many ways its structure is very similar. Its shaft is made up of two rods of spongy tissue— the *corposa cavernosa*—which, like the equivalent parts of the male penis, become filled with blood during sexual excitement. This makes the clitoris larger but not erect.

A man should be aware that the two *corpa cavernosa* bend backward and join the pelvic bones on either side of the vagina. They are covered over by muscles that contract during sexual excitement and restrict blood from leaving the clitoris. Another muscle joins the shaft of the clitoris underneath, and is the direct equivalent of the muscle that contracts during a man's climax and ejaculates semen out through his penis. As it passes back from the clitoris, this muscle divides in two and extends down each side of the vagina.

Now you can see why, physiologically, those gentle early stimulations of the lips of the vagina and the vagina itself can be more effective in arousing a woman toward orgasm than immediately attacking her clitoris. The muscles around the vagina contract, and not only provide pleasurable sensations in her vagina, but help to enlarge her clitoris and to tug on it as well.

Even today, despite the combined efforts of numerous qualified sexologists (myself included), persistent and widespread fallacies about the clitoris still remain. At least you can make sure that *you're* not taken in.

Let's take a quick rundown, and dismiss them one by one.

1. The size of a woman's clitoris is related to her sexual enjoyment. Not true—women's clitorides vary in size and shape in exactly the same way that men's penises vary in size and shape, and all women, properly stimulated, are capable of reaching a high peak of sexual pleasure.

2. Women need continuous clitoral stimulation in order to achieve orgasm. Not true—which makes some of the "clitoris-stimulating" attachments that some men wear around their penises look pretty damned pointless, to say the least. Just before a woman reaches orgasm, her clitoris actually withdraws, although rhythmical pressure on her clitoral area will continue to stimulate her, even when it's out of sight and direct touch.

3. Direct pressure on the clitoris is essential to excite a woman before making love. Not true—as one sexologist wrote: "When women masturbate—and most women do at some time or another—they hardly ever touch the glans of their clitoris directly. Many women do rub or press on the shaft of the clitoris, but most never do so. *Instead, they stimulate the clitoris indirectly* [my italics] by touching nearby parts. They may prefer pressure on the pubic mound, the swelling just above the vulva, or stroking the labia minora. To them, touching the clitoris itself may bring discomfort."

4. There are several different kinds of orgasm: vaginal, clitoral, and G-spot. Not true! Although orgasms may be brought about by different kinds of stimulation—clitoral, vaginal, anal, or even by stim-

ulation of the breasts—every orgasm is a manifestation of the same response—the spasm of the outer part of the vagina, which then results in a series of pleasurable rhythmic contractions.

Because of the widely varying ways in which a woman may have been aroused, because of the widely varying differences in atmosphere, surroundings, and how a woman feels about the man who has aroused her, orgasms certainly *feel* different. Just as women shed tears for many different reasons, it doesn't mean that there are different kinds of tears.

I have never read in any textbook that men's climaxes feel just as different as women's orgasms, but the fact is that they do. One climax might feel like an explosion in the head of the penis, another might feel as if it's being pumped out by deeply rooted muscles. Another climax might virtually flow out, with very little muscular spasm, before a man can stop it. Again, it depends on circumstances, and how that particular act of love has progressed. But the reality is that all male climaxes and all female orgasms are basically the same physical response.

All we are concerned about here is how to *intensify* that response.

As orgasm approaches, the clitoris stiffens, becoming hard and ridgelike—or "beaklike" as I once described it. But then it tends to withdraw, so that a man who has been skillfully masturbating his partner suddenly discovers (oops!) that he hasn't got much of a protrusion to masturbate. This *doesn't* mean that she's suddenly lost interest. It means the opposite—that she's very close to climaxing.

At this point, he should press two or three fingertips gently but firmly against the clitoral shaft, and massage her quickly and rhythmically in counterclockwise motion, perhaps exerting slightly more pressure with his middle finger than his other fingers. His thumb and his pinkie meanwhile don't have to be idle; they can be massaging the outer lips of her vulva, or tugging gently but insistently at her pubic hair.

The intensity and pleasure of a woman's orgasm can be increased to peak-performance levels if a man stimulates the muscle around the vaginal entrance, the same muscle that's attached to the shaft of the clitoris. He can do this during intercourse by swiveling his hips downward and backward while he thrusts, so that he pulls her vagina downward, while the head of his penis rubs even more insistently against her "G-spot"—in other words, the back of her deeply buried clitoris.

The Masterton Method

Or he can use the Masterton Method, which many hundreds of loving couples have helped me devise, and which is *guaranteed* to produce a more intensive climax for both partners. It's simple, but because it's simple it's much more effective than most orgasmic techniques. Not only will it give a woman all the intensity and wetness of a "G-spot" orgasm, but it will also intensify the man's climax, which the "G-spot" techniques manifestly failed to do.

As we have seen, peak-performance sex is achieved by mutual arousal and mutual satisfaction, and in the final analysis *both* partners should feel fulfilled.

The Masterton Method works best in the rear-entry position, in which the woman lies on her side and her lover enters her vagina from behind.

Let's assume that our ideal couple have flirted, kissed, wined and dined, and gone through all the preliminaries of undressing, going to bed (or wherever), and foreplay. They have reached the point of penetration and intercourse, and the man is slowly but steadily thrusting into his partner's vagina from behind.

This position has many advantages. To begin with, the man has his hands free, so that he can caress and stimulate his partner while his penis thrusts into her. In the jolly old man-on-top position, a man has to use his arms to lift his considerably heavier weight off the woman's body, and is physically unable to give her all the subtle ongoing stimulation that she deserves.

There are times when the man-on-top position is good, such as during loving, romantic fucks on Valentine's night. Outdoors, under the sky.

But if you're looking for really intense indoor orgasms, the rear-entry position has a lot more going for it, and will bring you orgasmic rewards that you never dreamed possible.

Anybody can use the Masterton Method. It's neither complicated nor difficult. But it *does* work. Out of 225 couples who tried it, fewer than four reported that "it made no difference . . . neither better nor worse." All of the remaining couples said that it had "given both of us a truly satisfying experience" . . . "the first world-class orgasm in *years*, believe me" . . . "a simultaneous climax, which we'd never experienced before" . . . "heaven, of a sort" . . . "ripples that never seemed to end."

As the man thrusts into his partner's vagina, he should gently lift her upper leg (depending on which side she's lying) and keep it raised by supporting it on his own leg. Then he should deepen his thrusts (rhythmically, strongly, but not violently . . . "with a *swinging* motion" as the late Dr. Robert Chartham used to describe it to me, during the time he worked for me on *Penthouse Forum*—an excellent description).

As the man deepens his thrusts, he should reach down with both hands and place four fingertips on each vaginal lip. Then he should part her lips wide (as wide as his partner will accept) and begin quickly to massage her left lip counterclockwise, her right lip clockwise, with light but persistent pressure— and a very slight emphasis on *downward* tugging.

A man should keep up this contra-rotating massage throughout the act of intercourse. It has several very distinct advantages over other methods of sexual stimulation. First, it involves *both* partners simultaneously. Second, it gives the man a very high degree of control over the timing of his climax. In the rear-entry position, he can lean backward in order to *increase* the stimulation of his partner's vagina on his penis, or forward in order to *lessen* it. He can also lessen the stimulation of his penis by gently pulling his partner's vaginal lips a little wider.

If the man feels that his climax is still approaching too quickly, he can easily withdraw his penis from his partner's vagina altogether, but continue to massage it against her vulva to maintain the intimacy and excitement of genital contact. In the rear-entry position the least-sensitive part of his glans is rubbing against her vulva, so this continuing massage is unlikely to bring him to climax.

By using the Masterton Method a man is *directly* stimulating not just her clitoris, but her vaginal entrance, too, both at the same time, because he is massaging the *bulbospongiosus*—the muscle that encircles the entrance to his partner's vagina, and that is also attached to the shaft of her clitoris. Steady, quick, sensitive massage will be rewarded by the swelling of her vaginal lips, the swelling of her clitoris, a flow of vaginal juice, and an orgasm that she will long remember him for.

An orgasm achieved by the Masterton Method

usually takes a little longer than an orgasm achieved through clitorial stimulation alone. But, according to those women who have tried it, it's well worth waiting for.

Twenty-five women out of thirty said that it was "at least 10 percent more satisfying than my usual orgasm." And all thirty said that they had enjoyed the act of intercourse more—principally because "it lasted longer, and I had plenty of time to become fully aroused."

Gina, a 28-year-old dancer from San Francisco, said: "I was always capable of reaching orgasm, but I was always slow to get turned on, and of course there aren't many men who have the skill or the patience to wait for you. I went through three long-term sexual relationships with men I really liked, and in each relationship I had to resort to masturbation after lovemaking, so that I could at least get rid of all my sexual tension.

"There are times during my menstrual cycle when I find it more difficult to reach orgasm than at other times. I can feel the orgasm rising in me, but just when I think I'm nearly there, it dies away again.

"But this method is excellent. It involves a very loving embrace, I love having a man hold me from behind. It's comfortable, and you have your hands free. I adored that rotating kind of massage. Sometimes he squashed my vaginal lips tight around the shaft of his penis . . . other times he stretched them wide apart. It gave me a very deep feeling between my legs, which was quite unlike any feeling I'd had before."

Loreen, a 46-year-old grade-school teacher from Houston, Texas, said: "I thought I'd gotten to an age when I couldn't expect shattering orgasms any longer. I'd been having a pretty bumpy time with my hormones; and at the age of 41 I'd had a partial hysterectomy, which solved my bleeding problems but didn't do anything to stabilize my emotions or my premenstrual tension. There are still times of the month when I can be pretty damn snappy.

"But Jake and I used this method. It seems so obvious when you try it, this slow continuous massage. Jake had touched me in a *similar* way before, but not so consistently, and not as a deliberate build-up toward orgasm. I was a long time coming, as you might say. But after about ten minutes or so, I began to realize that I *was* going to have an orgasm, and that it was going to be strong. When it did come, I almost blacked out . . . and the most amazing bonus was that Jake came, too, at one and the same time, the first time we'd enjoyed simultaneous orgasm in years.

"Jake said that he very much liked the control it gave him over his own climax, but more than that he liked the feeling that he knew exactly what to do to arouse me, and to give me the best time possible."

Above all, the secret of the Masterton Method is consistency of stimulation. During normal intercourse, the muscle around the vaginal entrance is tugged or massaged in just the same way, and this tugging is partly responsible for women achieving climaxes by the penetration of the penis alone. But few men, just by using their penis alone, can maintain the kind of steady, rhythmical, gradually strengthening massage that is almost guaranteed to bring a woman to orgasm.

Again and again, women have complained to me that "he just starts doing something I like . . . something that really gets me going . . . then he suddenly stops, and changes to another position, or runs out of steam . . . and all that stimulation just dies away."

Like any new sexual technique, the Masterton Method requires practice and patience—particularly in respect to the timing of the massage strokes, and how much pressure is applied to the vaginal lips. In order to get *these* exactly right, a woman will have to tell her lover what kind of speed and what kind of pressure she prefers. There's no harm in her saying, "Harder! Faster!" or "Harder! Slower!" or "Not so hard, not so fast," and so on.

Gina said, "It did take us a while to get it right." But so far the orgasmic response that it has achieved has shown it to be consistently more successful in giving women deep and satisfying orgasms than almost any other method of stimulation, including the rather questionable (and frequently futile) search for the "G-spot."

A couple who practice the Masterton Method on a regular basis will discover a new sexual intimacy, a heightened ability to respond to each other's sensory needs, and considerably greater sexual fulfillment and satisfaction. In other words they will be reaching toward the very peak of their performance.

Now, finally, here are four examples of couples who achieved peak performance in their sex lives—by self-education, by self-exploration, and by deciding that they wanted more variety when they went to bed.

If *you're* considering a dramatic change in your love life, you and your lover should sit down together and answer the following questions as candidly as you can.

DO YOU REALLY WANT
A MORE EXCITING SEX LIFE?

1. Are you interested in learning more about your own body and your own sexual responses?
2. Are you prepared to let your partner examine and touch your genitals as closely and for as long as he/she desires?
3. Would you consider touching and stimulating your own genitals in order to explore your own responses?
4. Would you agree to watch/look at sexually stimulating videos or magazines with your partner?
5. Would you dress (or undress) specifically to excite your partner sexually?
6. Are you interested in trying new methods of stimulating yourself and your partner?
7. Would you like your partner to spend more time on sexual foreplay (kissing, breast-caressing, etc.)?
8. Do you think you should spend more time on sexual foreplay?
9. Would you consider giving your partner more oral/genital stimulation?
10. Would you like your partner to give you more oral/genital stimulation?
11. Would you consider giving your partner more anal stimulation?
12. Would you like your partner to give you more anal stimulation?
13. Are you interested in getting yourself more physically fit for better sex?
14. Would you do sexual exercises (flexing perineal muscles, masturbation, etc.)?

15. Would you tell your partner your most arousing sexual fantasies?

16. Would you like your partner to tell you his/her most arousing sexual fantasies?

17. Would you consider acting those fantasies out—either partially or completely?

18. Would you shave your pubic hair specifically to excite your partner sexually?

19. Would you openly urinate in front of your partner, so that he/she could watch?

20. Would you be interested in making intimate sexual videos of each other?

21. Would you agree to try any sexual variation that your partner found exciting, such as mild bondage, the wearing of rubber or leather or Saran Wrap, or dressing in clothes of the opposite sex?

22. Are you prepared to tell your partner about your most secret sexual fantasies?

23. Are you prepared to ask your partner to play out all or part of your sexual fantasies for real?

24. Would you be willing to show your partner how you like best to be sexually stimulated?

25. Are you prepared to talk about your sexual feelings more openly with your partner than you have in the past?

These questions are not judgmental, so you don't need to worry about your score, although if you happened to answer yes to more than 20 of them, you obviously have the proper attitude about improving your sex life.

Primarily, these are guidelines to some of the avenues that you'll need to explore if you want to reach the peak of sexual performance. Sexual arousal—like any other kind of human stimulation—is very much a matter of taste. But unlike listening to music, for example, or eating exotic foods, sex has to be a matter of compromise between two people who may have extremely different ideas about what's arousing, what's acceptable, and what's a downright turn-off.

"Sex Used to Frighten Me"

As I mentioned at the very beginning of this book, an open-minded attitude toward your partner's sexual inclinations and his or her sexual inhibitions is absolutely essential if you are going to reach the peaks together.

You may have had a repressive upbringing, as far as sex is concerned. You may feel cautious or even frightened about trying new techniques in bed. You might find it almost agonizing to show your genitals openly, even to the person you love the most.

But the reassuring truth is that if your partner is somebody you love and trust, and who loves and trusts you in return, you have nothing to be afraid of but the explosive release of your own inhibitions, and the discovery that the truth about sex not only can make you free, but it can give you physical and emotional sensations beyond anything you thought possible.

The sexy people in this life aren't just the glamorous models and the society glitterati and the Hollywood pleasure seekers. Stunningly good sex is within everyone's reach—starting tonight.

Velma, a 36-year-old homemaker from Seattle, told me: "I don't know why sex frightened me so much. John kept wanting me to look at sex videos . . . they all seemed so lurid and vulgar. Women with huge breasts in black underwear, men with enormous bright-red penises. But after I read your last book I came to understand that it was the very vulgarity of it that stimulated him . . . that *all* men find that kind of thing stimulating—to a greater or lesser extent. I came to understand that John wasn't belittling me by wanting me to look at videos and magazines like that. He wasn't trying to tell me I wasn't sexy enough. He was simply trying to get me to participate in something that he got a kick out of, so that I could enjoy it, too . . . so that we could get excited together.

"I was brought up strict and religious, in a family where nobody saw anybody else in the bath, and the lessons I was given about the physical side of life were called 'sexual hygiene.' I still respect my parents and I'm still a deeply religious person. But God gave us minds and bodies to express our love for each other, and there's no wrong at all in expressing that love to the utmost.

"These days, I have quite a selection of sexy lingerie of my own, and if you really want to know I happen to own a vibrator, too. I don't feel depraved or corrupted in any sense at all. Our home life is happy and stable, and John and I have the finest family that anybody could wish for. I thank God for giving me so much joy in my marriage. I thank God for sexual love. And I bless all of those people, like you, who have fought for so long and so hard to make it possible for ordinary folks like us to experience our God-given gifts to the full.

"When I think that I might have gone to my grave not knowing such pleasure—well, that frightens me a whole lot more than sex ever did."

16

The Thrill of it All

These days, you can buy a whole selection of informative and open-minded sex manuals almost everywhere, and teachers, columnists, and celebrity therapists such as Dr. Ruth Westheimer are doing a great deal of hard and creative work on sexual education. But I still find time and time again that couples are cheating themselves in their sexual development because they're unable to make that final step toward total sexual communication.

It's frequently a result of plain old embarrassment and fear. How is he going to tell his well-brought-up childhood sweetheart, the mother of his children, the annual roaster of his Thanksgiving turkey, that he has a deep and burning fantasy to see her dressed in red stockings and a red garter belt and high heels and nothing else, with all of her pubic hair shaved off?

How is *she* going to tell her steady, reliable husband and provider, who commutes to the office every morning and comes back tired and hassled, the father and barbecue chef and Little League coach, that he always leaves her less-than-satisfied in bed, and that she would love him to lick her clitoris until she screams, and then give her three more orgasms on the bedroom rug?

He's frightened that his fantasies will shock her. She's frightened that her discontent will enrage him. With some justification, too. The most common response to a revelation that "you never wear sexy underwear" or "you never bother to make sure that I have an orgasm" is "why the hell didn't you tell me before?" accompanied by a great deal of shouting and disagreement.

The shouting and disagreement are understandable. They serve (a) to mask the couple's genuine frustration that the revelations didn't come earlier, (b) to mask their anger about not living up to their partner's sexual expectations, and (c) to mask their own embarrassment about what they have at last managed to reveal.

The shouting and the disagreement are usually followed by profuse apologies: "I didn't really mean you were *that* bad in bed, I was just making a point"—"I don't *really* expect you to wear black rubber if the idea of it turns you off." After which the couple's situation is in a worse state than it was before—they are still dissatisfied, still anxious about embarrassing or shocking one another, and still unable to communicate their sexual needs.

Sociologists are still asking, in this age of so-called sexual liberation, why so many long-term sexual relationships break up, why so many marriages dwindle and die, and why so many men and women are *still* anxiously seeking reassurance about their partner's sexual tastes and about their own sexual performance.

But the fact is that men and women are still very unskilled at communicating their sexual needs to each other. The prime symptom of this lack of communication is the dreaded and pathetic "war between the sexes," which, on the basis of broken relationships, appears to be growing worse rather than better. There has been an increasing trend for motion pictures and fiction to portray the sadistic treatment of women; and there has been a noticeable increase in hostility toward men from the women's movement.

You and your lover, however, can be the very distinct exceptions. You cannot only have the closest and most open sexual relationship of anybody you know—you can develop and improve it every single time you make love.

So many people regard sex as a repetitive, unchanging act. You feel thirsty this evening, you have a cold beer. You feel thirsty next Thursday evening, you have a cold beer. You feel thirsty on Sunday evening, you have a cold beer. But sex is not a simple thirst or a simple appetite. It's intellectual as well as instinctive, it's emotional as well as physical, and you need to nurture and develop and *change* your lovemaking as time goes by—otherwise it will become boring, unstimulating, and routine. In other words, you will have allowed it to become no more meaningful to your life than just another cold beer.

I asked a dozen couples—two who claimed to have an "excellent" relationship, seven who claimed to have a "fairly good" relationship, but three who had experienced some recent sexual difficulties—to follow the peak-performance sex plan.

I asked each couple to get together—to put their courage to the test—and to reveal themselves *totally* to their partner—to expose their bodies as intimately as possible—and to explain every single unfulfilled desire they might have been hiding.

To start with, they had to grant each other an unconditional sexual amnesty: whatever they said, whatever fantasies or criticisms they had, everything had to be accepted without anger or recrimination. "Why didn't you tell me that before?" was banned.

After only one month, eleven of the couples reported "really encouraging" changes in their sex lives. One couple regrettably split up, although they blamed a strong clash of personalities rather than their failed sex life.

Here is one of the most typical couples, and how they used the peak-performance sex plan to realign their relationship and become "infinitely" closer. *Fred is 22 years old and a business student at a Michigan university. He is tall, very athletic, and physically fit. He met Charlene three years ago when she was just 16. They started to live together a year ago in an apartment, which is paid for mainly by Charlene's salary as a department store beautician. Charlene is petite, blonde, and in Fred's words "Detroit's answer to Barbie."*

This is Fred's side of the story: "Charlene was very young and innocent when I first met her. I used to play college football in those days and she was one of the cheerleaders. I'd noticed her, you know, and thought she was pretty—but in those days I had a thing for dating older women. I guess I liked their confidence, you know, and their sophistication; and the fact that if they wanted to go to bed with you, they'd go to bed with you. You wouldn't have to spend three hours in the back seat of your friend's Corvette, trying to cajole some bundle of puppyfat out of her bra.

"But one night my current date Leanne stood me up for her husband of all people, so I guess out of revenge I went out with the first pretty girl I bumped into, which happened to be Charlene. I hadn't realized that Charlene had been following me around, starry-eyed, and that she had written my name about a thousand times in the back of her English folder.

"I took Charlene for dinner and then we went to a disco. She was so innocent and enthusiastic about everything compared with Leanne that I really enjoyed her company. I suddenly began to think that it was more fun to go out with somebody younger. I mean Leanne was great but she always made me feel as if I was ignorant; and when she made love she made love like she wasn't with me. You know, like she was alone. I might just as well have been one of those inflatable guys made out of pink plastic, you know the ones that frustrated spinsters use.

"Charlene knew zilch about sex but she was very sexy. Her parents were both real nice people. Her old man used to work for Ford and believed in honesty, decency, and hard work. The first time that Charlene and I ever made love was when her parents went to Chicago for the week. We had a hot necking session on the couch, and I slipped my hand into her blouse. She was wearing this little white cotton blouse, short-sleeved, I'll never forget it; and this short red pleated skirt, and white socks. Under her blouse her breasts were bare, she wasn't wearing a bra, the first time ever. Her breasts were a real turn-on. They're big, for a girl who's only five feet tall; but they're very high and firm, and the nipples tilt up.

"I fondled her breasts for a while, then I unbuttoned her blouse and took it off. She looked fabulous. Short blond pixie hair, bare breasts, pink nipples. And big wide eyes. I started to slide my hand up her skirt, but she clamped her thighs together and she wouldn't let me. I kissed her again and again, and I told her, 'I want to make love to you.' She said, 'I want to make love to you, too . . . just hold on.'

"She went through to her bedroom and would you believe she locked the door? I sat around drinking the rest of the wine and watching the Pistons on TV. After about a quarter of an hour Charlene opened her bedroom door and called me. Her bedcover was all turned down neat, her hair was brushed, and she was wearing this little pink nightshirt.

"She asked me if I wanted to turn off the light, but I said no way. She unbuttoned my shirt for me, and unbuckled my belt, but then she said 'I'll get into bed and wait for you.' I finished undressing and climbed into bed next to her. She said, 'You're only the second boyfriend I've ever been to bed with.' I said, 'At least I'm not the first . . . you'll be able to help me put this on.' I tore open a condom and pushed back the bedcover, and held my cock in my fist. I was real turned on and my cock must have looked huge. It was all wet, too. Fondling her breasts like that had really got me going.

"Charlene said, 'I can't do it, I don't know how.' But I said, 'Go ahead, roll it on,' and in the end she managed to stretch the condom over the head of my cock and start to unroll it. Her hands were shaking like crazy, but she did it. As soon as it was on, though, she snuggled down in the bed and covered me over with the quilt. She was so shy it was unbelievable, but she was so young and innocent I wasn't going to push her. Anyway, I liked it. I liked her being young and innocent. Leanne used to hunker down on top of me and pull the lips of her cunt open and tease me by bringing herself down just low enough to touch my cock, then lifting herself out of reach again. You wouldn't have caught Charlene doing anything like that!

"I lifted her nightshirt and kissed her breasts. She was soft and warm and she smelled so clean. She kissed me and stroked my back but she didn't touch my cock once. When I ran my hand down between her legs, her cunt was really wet. Soft wet fur, that's what it felt like. She shivered, kind of, but then I was eager to get inside her. I massaged her juice all around the knob of my cock, and then I pushed myself up into her cunt. It was hot. After Leanne, it was *very* tight. It was heaven. Always is!

"I thought: this young lady is really aroused. I'd never come across a girl so wet. And she was so small, too. I could fuck her real hard, really pump my cock into her. I heard her saying 'hard, Fred, hard,' and then I had a climax like an atom bomb, I swear. I lay back on that pillow and even *I* was panting, and I was totally fit. She was like nothing I'd ever experienced before.

"After that, we made love every possible opportunity we could. Charlene gradually grew out of her shyness, and after a while we started to laugh about the way she'd taken a shower that time and turned down the bed. She admitted that she had been embarrassed because her panties had gotten so wet. She had thought that I wouldn't like it, or else I might think she was oversexed, or that there was something wrong with her. I told her it was normal, almost all girls got wet panties when they were turned on, she just happened to get wetter than most.

"We used to go for drives and I'd slip one hand up her skirt and massage her cunt through her panties, making them wet on purpose. She used to pretend to struggle, but she really enjoyed it. It made her feel that she was grown-up now, I guess. She used to sit with her knees up, so that I could see up her skirt while I drove. There was just this one little white triangle of soaking-wet cotton that you could practically see right through, and her blond furry lips bulging out on either side. She was sexy as anything you ever saw. Maybe too much of a tease, if you want my feeling about it.

"Now—well, we've been living together for just over a year, and I don't know what's wrong. Charlene still hardly touches my cock when we make love . . . not that we seem to be making love too often these days. And for some reason all the excitement seems to have gone out of it. Sometimes I think about Leanne, and the way she used to prance around in her shoes and nothing else; and the way she used to push me back on the bed sometimes and suck my cock until the sperm dripped down her chin and *still* she wouldn't stop sucking. And when she was in the mood, Leanne used to love me fucking her from behind. She made me lie flat on my back on the bed, and then she'd walk around the bed, rubbing this perfumed lubricant stuff between the cheeks of her ass, and provoking me the whole time, saying things like 'You want it? You want it? Well . . . maybe I'll give it to you and maybe I won't.'

"Look at Us Joined Together"

But then she'd spread-eagle herself on top of me, with her back to me, and she'd writhe and wriggle around for a while. Then she'd take hold of my cock and massage it between her legs, up against her cunt. At last she'd lift her bottom up just an inch, and she'd fit the head of my cock into her anus, which was real tight, but it was slippery, too. She'd take a deep breath, and then she'd say, 'you dirty devil, you,' or something like that, or 'you bastard,' and she'd push herself down so that my cock slid into her ass all the way up to the balls. I wasn't allowed to move until she said I could. I mean that was one of the differences between my relationship with Leanne and my relationship with Charlene: Leanne gave all the orders.

"She'd take a hand mirror, and she'd hold it up so that we could both see in it. There were my balls, tight and wrinkled-up, and there was her anus stretched around the big hard shaft of my cock. I couldn't have gotten it up any further if I'd tried. 'Look at us joined together,' she used to say, and wriggle her ass. Then she'd give me the mirror, so that I could see what she was doing, and she'd pull the lips of her cunt apart, and press two fingers straight into that pink sticky hole of hers, and start rubbing my cock through the flesh of her cunt. She used to have some orgasms, believe me. Sometimes I thought she was never going to stop.

"She didn't care too much if I was satisfied or not. Like I said, she was only interested in me as a way of getting her rocks off. But when you've had sex like that, it's pretty hard to go back to one hundred percent straight fucking the way Charlene expects it. I tried to push my finger up Charlene's ass once, when we were right in the middle of doing it, and although she didn't say anything she clammed herself up tight, and believe me you couldn't have gotten a blade of grass up there, let alone a hard cock.

"As for oral sex, I've tried going down on her a few times but she always manages to twist herself around so that I can't reach her. And she sure hasn't shown any interest in giving me head."

So what was Fred's considered verdict about this sexual relationship with Charlene? He had initially described it as "fairly good," but after talking about it in detail he changed his mind and summed it up as "pretty much a disaster, on the whole. I think I would have gotten out of it months ago if I wasn't so fond of Charlene. Yes, I love her. But it's almost impossible to go on loving somebody if they're so damned inhibited that you can't show them how much."

Charlene, however, told a different story—and by reconciling their two points of view and bringing them together, their sexual difficulties were eventually overcome.

"Yes, I was very innocent about sex when I first slept with Fred. There was always gossip about sex around the schoolyard, and most of the time my friends and I talked about nothing but what 'it' would be like. But my family were very old-fashioned in their values and my mom and pop had both come from very strict homes themselves. I remember when I was about seven telling my grandma that I had to go for a leak and that practically brought the roof down.

"We had some pretty good sex education at school, but even though they taught us all of the biology and all about contraception and stuff they didn't explain how we were going to feel when we slept with boys, or how we were going to be able to *talk* about sex with our lovers or our husbands. Not being able to talk about sex was always my main problem with Fred.

"He was good about some things. Oh—he mentioned my wet panties, did he? He would! But he was good about that. He made me feel that something about which I was very embarrassed was sexy. I guess I kind of flaunted them after that, but he liked that, and if he liked it, then I liked it. Most of the time the problem was that I didn't know what he liked, what he wanted; and I was too inexperienced to be able to guess.

"The first time we made love I was very shy, but I tried to do everything properly. I can laugh at myself now because it wasn't exactly spontaneous, was it? But I'd read a book about 'the wedding night' and it said the bride ought to take a shower and put on a new nightdress and turn down the comforter and make the whole bedroom look inviting before the groom came to bed. I guess it was one of those books that was written in about 1901, huh?

"From that first night, though, I found Fred very violent during intercourse. One minute he'd be kissing me gently—the next minute he'd be feeling down between my legs to see if I was wet. Then it was straight in, bang, bang, bang. He used to shake me around like I was on a roller-coaster or something. Then bang, and that was it. He was finished. He climbed off me, and went to turn on the TV so that he could watch the Pistons. I should have called him the Piston himself, shouldn't I?

"I guess a lot of the problem was my fault. Fred just didn't seem to realize that he wasn't satisfying me at all. Because *he'd* got off, he thought that was the end of it. The trouble was, he kept talking as if he was keeping me so happy. He really seemed to believe that he was. He'd even put his arm around me in company and suggest that we had the most fulfilling sex life ever. But all that was happening was that he was making me more and more frustrated. He didn't seem to understand that—just because my panties got wet—I still needed a whole lot more to bring me to an orgasm. It takes me a long time to get aroused. I used to masturbate and sometimes it could take me twenty minutes or a half-hour or even longer. But another problem was that I didn't know how Fred could do that to me. I was embarrassed about masturbating, and I didn't realize that a man could do that to a woman—you know, with his fingers, and that it was still okay.

"I didn't tell Fred how I felt because I thought that I'd hurt his pride and that we'd probably break up. I love him, that's what made things worse, in a way. But I couldn't stand this shaking-about, this two minutes' grunting and groaning and then nothing. It got to the point where I began to hate sex and I almost began to hate Fred.

"One of the reasons I agreed to live with him is because I thought he'd learn to slow down if we lived together in our apartment, and didn't have to worry about my parents coming home or anything like that. But it didn't improve. In fact it got worse, and Fred started to get all angry and miserable too.

"When we sat down together for this peak-performance sex thing and talked out our needs and our desires and our fantasies—I have to tell you, it was like Christmas. That's all I can say. It was like all the lights were lit and the windows were flung open and the bells started ringing. When I understood that Fred was frustrated with me and Fred understood that I was frustrated with him, and *why*, well, we opened a bottle of champagne. Well, sparkling wine, that was all we had.

"It seemed so stupid that we hadn't talked to each other. But I could see why Fred hadn't wanted to tell me about Leanne and all that stuff. He was afraid I'd be disgusted, and jealous; and he was scared that I wouldn't want to try anything new. Just like I was afraid that he'd go crazy if I criticized his lovemaking, and leave me.

"I knew hardly anything about different sex like sucking a man's penis and things like that. We'd giggled about it at high school, but I didn't have the first idea how to go about it. Did you suddenly bend down and open your mouth and start sucking it? Were you supposed to suck it hard, like a Hoover, or what? I just didn't know, and because I didn't know I was scared to try.

"We chose an afternoon for our first session together, because Fred didn't have any lectures that day and I was free. I can't explain to you what I felt like. I was very nervous, very anxious . . . very afraid about telling Fred that he'd never once given me an orgasm in all the time we'd been sleeping together. But I'd read the books, at least I had a good knowledge of what a couple *could* do together, and at least I knew how to suck a man's penis without sucking it clean off!

"I'd spread out some big cushions in the living room, and Fred had propped up two large mirrors so that we could see ourselves clearly. We undressed and it was incredible, but we were both so shy with each other! We were like two people who had never seen each other naked before.

"Fred started first, and sat on a cushion in front of the mirror. He had a huge erection . . . almost as if he were expecting something terrifically sexy to happen. He showed me the glans, and the opening, and how he liked it to be touched. I asked him to show me how he touched his own penis, and it was fascinating to watch the very loose, quick way he masturbated, using all his penis and rubbing the top of his glans with his thumb. Then I had a try . . . and he had to ask me to stop because he was getting a little too close to a climax.

"He showed me how to stroke his balls without hurting them. Then came the big moment! I kissed his glans and licked all around it, and he showed me just how he liked to have his penis sucked. Well . . . it was more like lapping and kissing than sucking. I sucked his shaft, too, and took his balls into my mouth. All the time he kept whispering how much he loved me.

"He said we could leave the anal bit until later . . . but I said that if he could do it to me then I could do it to him. I smeared jelly onto my fingers, and he opened his legs wide so that I could slide my finger up his ass. It was difficult at first, because he wasn't too happy about it, and so his anus was really tight. But after a while I told him, 'Relax . . . relax . . . it tells you to relax,' and so he did. I was able to push two fingers up his ass and feel where his prostate gland was. I massaged it a few times and right in front of my eyes his penis started to pour out this clear juice.

"This time I wasn't shy. I put my mouth around it and sucked it up.

"Then it was my turn. Fred fondled my breasts and my nipples and I showed him I liked to have my nipples gently pinched and twisted . . . not too hard, but enough to make them stiffen up. Then I opened my legs in front of the mirror and together we located my vagina and my vaginal lips and my urethra and my clitoris. I could see myself in the mirror, looking hot from anxiety and embarrassment. But then Fred said, 'That's beautiful . . . show me how you like to touch it.'

"Never in my life had I ever admitted to anybody that I masturbated, let alone *done* it in front of anybody, in broad daylight, with my legs wide apart. But I did . . . and Fred watched me, and learned how to touch me in exactly the same way, exactly the way I liked it. In fact, he carried on masturbating me, on and on, and I lay back and let him do it, stretching my legs wider and wider. I knew that after what I'd told him that it was real important for him to make me come . . . and why should I stop him?

"His fingers flew and flew and when they went slightly off target I gently took hold of his wrist and guided him back again and he didn't mind. Then suddenly I knew that I couldn't stop myself coming. My legs squeezed together and I lay on my side and almost shook myself to pieces.

"Almost at once, Fred laid me on my back, and knelt between my legs, and slid his penis right up me. I had some aftershocks, and I clung to his arms and practically cried. He made love to me so slow, so hard, so gentle, relishing every single stroke. When he came, he shot the first big spurt up inside me . . . then he took his penis a little way out and shot the rest of his sperm on to my pubic hair. Then he lay on the cushion beside me, and slowly rubbed it in, touching my clitoris in exactly the right way.

"To begin with, I don't think either of us found the peak-performance sex plan very easy. Learning to touch Fred properly, learning how to love him physically, that wasn't difficult at all. The hardest thing of all is learning how to say to your partner, 'I love you, and whatever you want to do, I want to know about it'—and then accepting it and trying it when your partner *does* tell you . . . that's the most difficult thing to do.

"But that's what made the difference. You should see the way we make love now!"

Epilogue

Eighteen Ways You
Can Reach Your Peak Tonight

And finally, here are some sexual tricks you can do *tonight* to start you on your journey toward peak-performance sex. Good luck, good loving—and let me know how you get on.

1. Go out together and buy some hardcore magazines and a couple of hardcore videos. Take them into the bedroom. Give each one a score and see which turns you on the most.
2. Undress, and take turns slowly massaging each other with a little scented oil. Pay particular attention to each other's genitals.
3. Slowly masturbate together for three minutes only, then masturbate each other for the next three minutes, then go back to self-masturbation, and so on. Watch closely to see how your partner pleasures him/herself, and learn.
4. Give each other oral sex for three minutes in turn, then swap over, and so on. Give your partner guidance as to which oral caresses you like the most.
5. Buy some sex toys together—at least two each. Use them and see how you like them.
6. Swap fantasies, and act out those that appeal to you and turn you on.
7. Lie side by side and exercise your "sex-muscles" between your legs as strongly and as

rhythmically as you can. Women should try to push a vibrator out of their vaginas, then draw it back in again, then have their partners assist them in replacing it when it comes out.

8. Dress up in whatever erotic clothing your partner wants you to.

9. Take turns being each other's slave for a morning. During that morning, the slave must remain naked and perform whatever sexual or other services the master or mistress demands. There can be no refusals!

10. Masturbate together as fast as you can, until you both climax. Then see if you can masturbate each other even faster.

11. Make love anywhere but in the bedroom tonight.

12. Take a bath together tonight, and spend a long time washing each other, washing each other's hair, and then shaving each other's pubic hair.

13. As the water runs out, pee over your lover's genitals, and caress each other with your fingers.

14. Make love as slowly as you possibly can. You have all the time in the world.

15. Do one sexual thing for your partner that you have never done before (even if you never do it again). A mild spanking? A little polite bondage? Swallowing, when you never swallowed before?

16. Start a sex diary—one partner—and at the end of your first month compare notes. Remember, be totally honest; record the failures as well as the successes.

17. Resolve never to think about anything erotic again without telling your partner about it.

18. Resolve that you and your partner will put everything you've got into your sex life, and that you'll reach your sexual peak every single time you make love.

There's an epidemic with 27 million victims. And no visible symptoms.

It's an epidemic of people who can't read.

Believe it or not, 27 million Americans are functionally illiterate, about one adult in five.

The solution to this problem is you... when you join the fight against illiteracy. So call the Coalition for Literacy at toll-free **1-800-228-8813** and volunteer.

Volunteer Against Illiteracy. The only degree you need is a degree of caring.